Instant ไทย

How to Express 1,000 Different Ideas With Just 100 Key Words and Phrases

by Stuart Robson & Prateep Changchit

TUTTLE PUBLISHING
Tokyo • Rutland, Vermont • Singapore

Published by Tuttle Publishing, an imprint of Periplus Editions (Hong Kong) Ltd., with editorial offices at 364 Innovation Drive, North Clarendon, Vermont 05759, and 130 Joo Seng Road #06-01, Singapore 368357

Copyright © 2007 by Periplus Editions (Hong Kong) Ltd.

LCC Card Number: 2006938499
ISBN-13: 978-0-8048-3375-2
ISBN-10: 0-8048-3375-3

Distributed by

North America, Latin America & Europe
Tuttle Publishing
364 Innovation Drive
North Clarendon, VT 05759-9436 U.S.A.
Tel: 1 (802) 773-8930
Fax: 1 (802) 773-6993
info@tuttlepublishing.com
www.tuttlepublishing.com

Asia Pacific
Berkeley Books Pte. Ltd.
130 Joo Seng Road #06-01
Singapore 368357
Tel: (65) 6280-1330
Fax: (65) 6280-6290
inquiries@periplus.com.sg
www.periplus.com

12 11 10 09 08 07   6 5 4 3 2 1

Printed in Singapore

TUTTLE PUBLISHING® is a registered trademark of Tuttle Publishing, a division of Periplus Editions (HK) Ltd.

Contents

Preface

This little book aims to introduce the Thai language. It is intended for those who know nothing about it, but are keen to learn. We use the method of selecting 100 key words, and using these to make up sentences and present a range of expressions, so that you can "say 1000 things."

The words are arranged as ten topics, ones that will be helpful for the various situations you might find yourself in when visiting Thailand, traveling about and meeting Thai people. The language used is authentic, and contains many clues about Thai culture and society. There are also grammatical and cultural notes to help clarify things. An English-Thai wordlist gives the same vocabulary, but in reverse order, so that you can refer to it like a mini dictionary.

To help with the pronunciation we give the Thai in a simple system of romanization. Many systems exist. Ours is not meant to be scientific, merely useful for speakers of English. Thai script has also been inserted, so that Thai friends can help you to get the sounds right, and of course later on you might want to learn to read it yourself.

The Thai language is very different from English. But it is the key to learning about the people and culture of this fascinating country. So we would like to encourage you to have a go, use some Thai, and have the satisfaction of communicating successfully in this wonderful language.

Chork dii! Good luck!
Stuart Robson and Prateep Changchit

About the Thai language

Thai is the official language of the Kingdom of Thailand, and as such it is used by about sixty-five million people. It is taught and spoken over the whole country. Standard Thai is based on the language of the capital, Bangkok, as used by educated people.

Not surprisingly, there are several varieties of Thai, to be found in various parts of the country, namely:

- Central Thai, found in the central plain, and including Bangkok
- North-eastern Thai, also called Lao as it borders on Laos; many speakers of this variety come to Bangkok to work
- Northern Thai, centred on the ancient city of Chiangmai; and
- Southern Thai, found in peninsular Thailand, where the main centre is Nakhon Si Thammarat.

The differences between these varieties are significant, involving different tones and different vocabulary, but are not enough to warrant calling them separate languages. Sharing regional forms of the language brings a sense of identity, and most people are proud to use them when they meet others from the same area. The regional varieties of Thai are not normally written (only spoken); to write them would involve changing the tones and hence the spelling. The standard written language reflects the pronunciation and style of central Thailand and the capital, the center of government. As well as regional variants, there are of course also differences in speech depending on a person's social class or educational level.

As well as Thai in its several forms, we must not forget that there are other languages spoken within the borders of the country, such as:

- Malay, an important Austronesian language, found in the four southernmost provinces, bordering on Malaysia
- Karen, a Sino-Tibetan language, spoken by several groups in the mountains along the Burmese border
- Lisu, Akha, Lahu, Hmong and Yao, also Sino-Tibetan languages spoken in the mountainous parts of the north; and
- Khmer (or Cambodian), an Austroasiatic language, spoken in an area bordering on northern Cambodia.

This raises the question of ethnicity. Communities speaking these non-Thai languages are of course Thai in the sense of being subjects of the King, although they may not participate to the same extent in mainstream Thai culture, and may prefer to keep their own linguistic and cultural identity. Foreign visitors often enjoy traveling to see these "hill tribes" and their culture.

Thai belongs to a language-family called Tai. This includes Thai and its neighbor and close relative Lao, as well as Tai Yai or Shan, spoken in parts of northern Myanmar, Zhuang, a major language of southern China, Nung or Black and White Tai spoken by ethnic minorities in northern Vietnam, and the extinct Ahom found as far west as Assam in north-east India.

Thai entered the present Thailand only comparatively recently (11th and 12th centuries) from the north, and in this process came into contact with the Khmer and Mon who were already living there. As a result of this contact, we find many Khmer loanwords in present-day Thai. Some examples are:

tamruat	ตำรวจ	policeman
gamlang	กำลัง	strength
dtlaat	ตลาด	market
taleh	ทะเล	sea

There are also a large number of loanwords based on Pali (the sacred language of Theravada Buddhism) and Sanskrit (the ancient language of India), coined for the purpose of creating the terms needed for modern life, e.g.

thohrasap	telephone
sukhaphaap	health
wattanatham	culture

And there are many more taken directly from English, e.g.

thiiwii	TV
sehrok	photocopy (xerox!)
chek bin	may I pay the bill?
hoten	hotel
bai-bai	bye-bye!

Basic Thai is monosyllabic, and loanwords all seem to have two or more syllables. You can see that certain sounds have been changed in the process of adoption into the Thai language.

Thai is a tonal language. In other words, the pitch on which a word is pronounced can be important, as it may distinguish it from another, similar, word with a different pitch. There are five tones. Tones are inherent, that is to say, they are a "built-in" element of the word. When you learn Thai you have to learn the tone of each word—this is not something you can put off till a later date (on tones, see pages 18–20). In fact, there are rules related to the form and spelling of words that help you to predict what their tone will be. By the way, Thai is not related to Chinese or Vietnamese, which also happen to be tonal.

Thai has its own script (or writing system), that was developed in the 13th century to write its particular sounds, and is based on Khmer script. This system is basically syllabic (not actually an alphabet), and is related not only to Khmer and Cham script, but also Burmese, Javanese and Balinese scripts, all of which derive ultimately from a script used in South India in the early common era (A.D.), and which was brought into Southeast Asia with the spread of Indian civilization, which included Buddhism and Hinduism and their scriptures.

It is possible to represent the sounds of Thai in the familiar Western script (called roman), although there are a few problems with this, and various methods have been used. We have attempted to devise a system that is not only accurate but also not too difficult for the beginning student to understand and read (please see 12–18). We also include the Thai script for each item in this book, so that Thai friends can help you with pronunciation (Thais are generally not familiar with a romanization of their language).

Note that Thai has its own "alphabetical" order, which you will need to learn if you want to master Thai script and use a Thai-English dictionary.

Spelling and Pronunciation

This section aims to show the spelling system that we have adopted for this book and, where necessary, to explain how to pronounce the letters and combinations of letters. This system is in fact not a transliteration, in the sense that one Thai sign is always represented by one roman letter, and it thus does not attempt to reproduce the spelling of Thai (as found in the Thai script). It is hoped that the method used will be clear and helpful for English-speaking readers.

To facilitate the discussion, we look first at the consonants, and then at the vowel sounds, giving an example word and the Thai spelling. The pronunciation is as in English, except where indicated otherwise.

Consonants

g   **gài**   ไก่   chicken

kh   **khài**   ไข่   egg
the *k* has aspiration (wind behind it); it could also be written with just *k*.

ng   **nguu**   งู   snake
This is the same sound as the *ng* in "si<u>ng</u>"; when it comes at the beginning of a word, it may be hard to say. Try saying "singer," then slowing it down and

breaking it into two parts: "si-nger." Then you can get *ng* in an initial position.

j	**jaan**	จาน	plate
ch	**chórn**	ช้อน	spoon
s	**sìi**	สี่	four
d	**dèk**	เด็ก	child
dt	**dtaa**	ตา	eye

This sound and the following sound have to be carefully distinguished. This is like a *t* but with no wind behind it. You can get this effect by pursing the lips before releasing the sound.

th	**Thai**	ไทย	Thai

This is a *t* with wind behind it; it is never the *th* of "th̲ing."

n	**norn**	นอน	to lie down
b	**bâan**	บ้าน	house
bp	**bplaa**	ปลา	fish

This sound and the following sound also have to be carefully distinguished. This one is like a *p*, but with no wind behind it. Again, to get it right you have to purse the lips before releasing it.

ph   **phâa**   ผ้า   cloth

This sound is an ordinary *p*, but with wind behind it. It is never *ph* as in "p̲h̲oto" (we have another letter for the *f* sound).

f	**fan**	ฟัน	tooth
m	**man**	มัน	it
y	**yaa**	ยา	medicine
r	**rórn**	ร้อน	hot, temperature
l	**lom**	ลม	wind
w	**wát**	วัด	temple
h	**hông**	ห้อง	room

plus a glottal stop that is not normally written (but has a role in pronunciation) and will be represented with an apostrophe when needed.

Vowels

Apart from the differences between tones (to be discussed on page 18), there is also an essential difference between long and short vowels. To mark this, we simply write the vowel sound double—that is, it has to be sounded as longer than the short one.

a   **wan**   วัน   day

The example sounds like English "won." The *a* is like the *a* in "h<u>a</u>!" It is never the *a* of English "c<u>a</u>t" (this exists as well, though—see page 16).

aa   **maa**   มา   to come

This could be written *ah*; the example word sounds like English "mar," but of course without any *r* attached to it.

i   **prík**   พริก   chilli

This is a short sound, as in English "<u>i</u>f."

ii   **mii**   มี   to have

This is the long version of the above; think of the *ee* in "s<u>ee</u>."

u   **khun**   คุณ   you *(polite)*

This is the short sound as found in English "f<u>oo</u>t" or "p<u>u</u>t."

uu **nguu** งู snake

This is the long version of the above, like the *oo* in English "m__oo__d."

The next group of sounds is a little more difficult:

oh **giloh** กิโล kilo

This is the *o* of English "g__o__," to be carefully distinguished from the next two sounds.

o **lom** ลม wind

As in English "fr__o__m."

or **lor** หล่อ handsome

The sound intended here is the English *or*, but without any "r" attached to it; it could also be represented with *aw*, as in "__aw__ful."

eu **meu** มือ hand

There are short and long versions of this sound. It is like the *eu* of French "d__eu__x," but tighter. Compare *oe* below.

ae **lae'** และ and

This is the *a* sound of "c__a__t." Note the glottal stop on the end, making the sound short.

e   **lék**   เล็ก   small
This is just the *e* of English "met."

eh   **mehk**   เมฆ   cloud
This is like the *e* acute of French, rather than English
ay; it could also be written with *air* (no "r" sound
attached), but is a pure vowel, not a diphthong.

oe   **thoe**   เธอ   you (familiar pronoun)
Like the *ir* of "bird" (no "r" attached); or the *ö* of
German. There are long and short versions.

Next, there is a wonderful array of diphthongs, that is,
combinations of two (or more) vowels. The sounds are
as indicated above, but run together, as follows:

ia	**mia** [pronounce like *mee-ah*]	เมีย	wife (*informal*)
iu	**hǐu** [*hew*]	หิว	hungry
eua	**reua** [*rer-ah*]	เรือ	boat
ua	**wua** [*woo-ah*]	วัว	cow
ai	**yài** [rhymes with *hi*!]	ใหญ่	big

ao	**mau** [*mow*, rhymes with *wow!*]	เมา	drunk
ui	**khui** [*kooy*]	คุย	to chat
oi	**noi** [*noy*]	น้อย	a little
oei	**khoei** [*ker-y*]	เคย	ever
euai	**nèuai** [*ner-ay*]	เหนื่อย	tired
io	**dio** [*dee-oh*]	เดียว	alone
eho	**leho** [*lay-oh*]	เลว	bad
aeo	**maeo** [*mair-oh*]	แมว	cat
iau	**nĭau** [*nee-ow*]	เหนียว	sticky

Tones

This is an especially interesting feature of the Thai language, one that gives it a pleasant "singing" sound. The tones are essential, as mentioned above, and not an optional extra. Every Thai word can be said to have a tone, that is, has to be pronounced on a particular pitch. Changing the tone may, in some cases, produce a different word—sometimes with amusing or embarrassing results.

There are five tones in Thai. We call them:

- mid
- high
- falling
- low, and
- rising.

We have marks to indicate these. Each one has its typical contour.

The majority of words are **mid tone**, so no mark is used for them. When pronouncing a **mid tone**, we have to be careful to hold the note steadily, not let it drop or rise.

The **high tone** starts higher than mid, and rises to a little "hook" at the end.

The **falling tone** starts high, and then drops.

The **low tone** sounds like an English emphatic tone: "No!"

The **rising tone** starts low and then goes up.

Native speakers of Thai have very sharp ears for these differences, and so in natural speech the distinctions are sometimes minimal, and may be slurred over when words are in combination. But the learner is well advised to produce the tones exactly, and even to exaggerate them, in order to hit the right note. You can practice by "conducting" with your hand in the air.

In some of the example words already given, some tone marks can already be seen; a complete set looks like this:

Bpaa	ปา	throw	(mid tone)	¯
Bpàa	ป่า	forest	(low tone)	`
Bpâa	ป้า	aunt	(falling tone)	^
Bpáa	ป๊า	father (Chinese)	(high tone)	´
Bpǎa	ป๋า	father (Papa)	(rising tone)	ˇ

Please note that when a vowel sound is written with two letters, the mark is placed over the first, but this of course applies to both.

PART 1

Words 1–10

Getting to know you

People traveling in Thailand will obviously want to become better informed about everything they see about them and will seek social contact with Thais. The best way to make contact is to exchange a few words in Thai. Your Thai friends will be pleased, and will help you with the pronunciation.

1 DII ดี

Dii! ดี Good! Right! Okay!

Dii măi? ดี ไหม Is that okay? Do you agree?

We have already found out how to make a question: the word **măi** ไหม is placed after the thing being questioned.

Sawatdii. สวัสดี Hello!
This is an all-purpose word of greeting. It can be used

with anybody, and at any time of day. Informally, people just say **Watdii!** หวัดดี. You can use it to say "hello" on the phone, and also to say goodbye. (It isn't actually derived from **dii** ดี at all, but is useful to include here.)

Sabai dii măi? สบายดีไหม Are you well?

To answer a question like this, just repeat the main word (without the question word):

Sabai dii. สบายดี Yes, I am.

Chohk dii โชคดี Good luck.

Yin dii. ยินดี It's my pleasure.

Yin dii thîi rúujak. ยินดี ที่ รู้จัก Nice to meet you.

Dii jai. ดีใจ Happy (to see you, know you; literally "good in my heart").

But if you turn the words around, you get a different meaning: **Jai dii** ใจดี kindhearted.

Grammatical Notes

1. Thai words don't change their form for tense (as English **take—took**), or number (house-houses) and so on, but word-order is very important. If the order is changed, this will probably change the meaning.

2. Qualifying words follow the thing qualified, as we see with **dii** ดี here, coming after **jai** ใจ, and so on.

3. Some words have a second meaning, just as English ones do. You will discover these as you progress.

4. Thai prefers to leave out "unnecessary" words, provided the sentence is clear, so there may be nothing for "it," "I" etc., although they do need to be supplied in translation.

2 CHÊU ชื่อ name

Khun chêu arai. คุณชื่ออะไร What is your name?

Phŏm chêu Simon. ผมชื่อไซมอน My name is Simon.

Chăn chêu Helen. ฉันชื่อเฮเลน
My name is Helen.

Kău chêu Richard. เขาชื่อ ริดชาร์ด
His name is Richard.

Khun mii chêu lên măi? คุณมีชื่อเล่นไหม

Do you have a nickname?

Grammatical Notes

The word **chêu** ชื่อ can be translated into the English word "name" or with the verb "to be called."

We see here a selection of useful pronouns. The word **khun** คุณ here functions as a second person pronoun, "you," and is polite—you can use it for someone you don't know very well yet. There are other possibilities: **thoe** เธอ, for someone you know well, or **thâan** ท่าน, which is suitable for someone in a high position or who deserves respect.

For "I" we have **phǒm** ผม (man speaking), and **chǎn** (informal) ฉัน or **dichǎn** (formal) ดิฉัน (woman speaking). For "we" we have **rau** เรา .

The word **khǎu** เขา means "he" or "she"—Thai makes no distinction for gender here. There is also no distinction for number—**khǎu** เขา is also used for "they."

Cultural Notes

Thai people have a first name and a surname or family name. But the custom differs substantially from the Western one: the surname is used only for official purposes. (Sometimes this name is long and impressive, and people have difficulty remembering others' names.) It is the "first" name, or **chêu jing** ชื่อจริง

("real" name) that is used in daily life, often with the title **Khun** คุณ in front of it, meaning Mr, Mrs or Miss (not to be confused with **khun** คุณ, "you"). Thai people tend to extend this usage to Western friends, so you may get called **Khun John** คุณ จอห์น ("Mr John") and so on, when Thais are talking to you or about you. It sounds friendly, but it's respectful too.

As well as these two names, people always have a **chêu lên** ชื่อเล่น ("play name") or nickname. This is used in the family or among close friends. Such names are short and sometimes humorous, e.g. **Nók** นก "Bird," or **Mǔu** หมู "Pig," as well as others that are harder to translate. Otherwise the name is just the last syllable of the first name. The nickname is never used for official purposes.

▇3▇ PHÓP GAN พบกัน to meet

Phóp gan mài. พบกันใหม่
We'll meet again (= See you later).

Phóp gan iik khráng. พบกันอีกครั้ง
I'll see you another time.

Phóp gan thîi nǎi? พบกันที่ไหน
Where will we meet? (Where will I meet you?)

Phóp gan mêua-rai? พบกันเมื่อไหร่
When will we meet?

Note

The word **gan** กัน means "together, with each other," and can occur in other expressions, such as **rák gan** รักกัน, "to love each other."

4 RÚU-JÀK รู้จัก to know, be acquainted

Khun rúu-jàk Mali măi? คุณ รู้จักมะลิ ไหม
Do you know Mali?

Thoe rúu-jàk rong-raem Oriental măi?
เธอรู้จัก โรงแรม โอเรียลต์ไหม
Do you know the Oriental Hotel?

Mâi rúu-jàk. ไม่รู้จัก No, I don't.

Grammatical Notes

Although they may look similar, **măi** ไหม and **mâi** ไม่ are different words: they have different tones and different positions in a sentence.

1. **măi** ไหม (rising tone) marks a sentence as a question, and always comes last;

2. **mâi** ไม่ (falling tone) is the sign of the negative ("no, not") and always comes in front of the word it negates;

3. and there is yet another one, **mài** ไม่ (low tone) that we met earlier, with a meaning "again, more."

5 YÙU อยู่
to be there, present; to live, dwell

Khun Wichaa yùu mǎi? คุณ วิชา อยู่ ไหม
Is Mr Wichaa there? (= Is Mr Wichaa in?)

Tim yùu thîi nǎi? ทิม อยู่ที่ไหน
Where is Tim?

Tim yùu thîi bâan. ทิมอยู่ที่บ้าน
Tim is at home.

Bâan gèut yùu thîi nǎi? บ้านเกิด อยู่ ที่ไหน
Where is your home town ("village of birth")?

Chǎn yùu thîi Melbourne. ฉันอยู่ที่ เมลเบอร์น
I live in Melbourne.

For a different meaning of **yùu** อยู่, see Word 7 below.

6 MÂI ไม่ no; not

Mâi! ไม่ No! Don't!
(There is also another word for "don't," **yàa** อย่า.)

Mâi sabai. ไม่สบาย (I'm) not feeling well.

Mâi dii. ไม่ดี
(That's) not good (not a good thing, not a good idea).

Mâi au. ไม่เอา
I don't want it (I won't accept it, literally "not take").

Mâi chôrp. ไม่ชอบ (I) don't like it.

Mâi sǒnjai. ไม่สนใจ (I'm) not interested.

Mâi sǔay. ไม่สวย
(It's) not beautiful. (I don't find it attractive.)

Mâi bpen rai. ไม่เป็นไร
No worries! It's okay! It doesn't matter! Not at all!

This last expression represents a cultural value in Thailand, namely that we shouldn't take things too seriously, but accept what can't be changed and carry on.

The word **rai** ไร is a shortened form of **arai** อะไร "what; anything." Some Thais pronounce the "r" ร as an "l" ล in informal speech, so be prepared for this.

7 THAM ทำ to do; to make

Khun tham arai? ? คุณทำอะไร
What do you do? *Or* What are you doing?

Chăn tham ahăan. ฉันทำอาหาร
I'm cooking (literally "making food").

Phŏm tham-ngaan. ผมทำงาน
I'm working. (literally "doing work")

Phŏm duu tiiwii yùu. ผม ดูทีวีอยู่
I'm watching TV.

Chăn norn lên yùu. ฉันนอนเล่นอยู
I'm taking a nap.

Chăn shopping yùu. ฉัน ชอบปิ้งอยู่
I'm shopping.

Here the word **yùu** อยู่ comes in a final position, and says "in the process of," "engaged in," like the English present continuous tense.

8 LÁEW แล้ว already; past tense marker

Sèt láew. เสร็จแล้ว It's finished (has been done).

Mòt láew. หมดแล้ว It's all used up (finished).

Jàai láew. จ่ายแล้ว (I've) paid already.

Khâu-jai láew. เข้าใจแล้ว
I understand (literally "understand already").

Fǒn dtòk láew. ฝนตกแล้ว
It's raining (has started to rain).

Grammatical note

This is a very important word. It is the only way we can express a past tense in Thai. But we don't always need to translate it with a past tense, as the examples show, if it is already clear that the process is complete or the condition has been achieved. It always comes in a final position. See also the next word.

9 YANG ยัง not yet; still

Gin yaa láew yang? กินยาแล้วยัง
Have you taken the medicine yet?
(literally "already or not yet").

Gin láew กินแล้ว I have … .

Phóp Khun Fernando rĕu yang?
พบคุณ เฟอร์นานโด หรือยัง
Have you met Fernando yet?

Yang. ยัง Not yet.

Khău yang yùu thîi Chumporn. เขายังอยู่ที่ชุมพร
He's still in Chumporn.

🔟 KHRÁP; KHÀ
(no translation) polite particles

These two words should be introduced at an early stage, because they are very common. They are found at the end of a sentence, and they serve to make it sound polite (less blunt). The interesting thing about them is the gender difference:

Khráp ครับ is said only by men, and
Khà ค่ะ is said only by women.

This is the rule.

There is another way they can be used, however. This is alone, as a one-word sentence. Here they still express politeness, and can be translated with "yes" (=I agree, I have heard what you said, and will act on it).

By the way, Thai does have another word for "yes," but it is very informal, a bit like the English "mm"; we could spell it **êr**… (with a falling tone).

Cultural note

Under the heading of "Meeting and greeting" we have to mention a gesture, the famous Thai **wâai** ไหว้. This consists of placing the palms of the hands together in front of the chest.

Whereas Westerners or people from the Middle East shake hands as a greeting, the Thais use the **wâai** ไหว้ to say hello and goodbye. It is the polite thing to do, and it is much appreciated if the visitor does it.

There is a certain "protocol" for making the **wâai** ไหว้, bearing in mind its function, namely to express respect. So we **wâai** ไหว้ "up," to someone we want to show respect to, including a new acquaintance. If someone makes a **wâai** ไหว้ to you, you must return it (if you're carrying something, then one hand will do, or even just a little bow). Consequently, you do not make a **wâai** ไหว้ to a younger or junior person first (but you do return it), and of course you never make one to a child.

Curiously, according to Thai custom we do not make a **wâai** ไหว้ to a member of the royal family. Instead we would bow (if a man) or curtsy (if a woman), if we had the privilege of being introduced to one.

PART 2

Words 11–20

Asking questions and getting answers

11 ARAI อะไร what?

Nîi arai? นี่อะไร What is this (close by)?

Nîi nangsěu. นี่ หนังสือ This is a book.

Nân arai? นั่น อะไร What is that (further away)?

Nân wát. นั่น วัด That's a temple.

An níi arai? อันนี้อะไร What is this (item)?

An níi nangsěu deun-thaang. อันนี้หนังสือเดินทาง
This is a passport.

An nán arai? อันนั้นอะไร What is that (item)?

An nán grabpǎu. อันนั้น กระเป๋า
That is a bag (piece of baggage).

Grammatical note

You may have detected the difference in tone between **nîi** นี่ and **níi** นี้. This is because they have a different function, even though both have been translated with "this." When it stands by itself as a sort of pronoun ("this something") then it is pronounced **nîi** นี่, but when it describes (and follows) a noun, then it is pronounced **níi** นี้. This means that in the above examples the word **an** อัน is a noun. In fact it is a useful little word, "thing."

12 THÎI NǍI ที่ไหน where?

Khun yùu thîi nǎi? คุณอยู่ที่ไหน
Where do you live?

Phǒm yùu thîi Grungthêhp. ผมอยู่ที่กรุงเทพ
[usually spelled Krungthep] I live in Bangkok.

Bâan khun yùu thîi nǎi? บ้านคุณอยู่ที่ไหน
Where is your house/home?

Thîi thanǒn Sukhumwit. ที่ ถนน สุขุมวิท
In Sukhumwit Road.

Khun jà' bpai thîi nǎi? คุณจะไปที่ไหน
Where are you going (where will you go)?

Phǒm jà' bpai thîi rong-raem. ผม จะไปที่โรงแรม

I'm going to the hotel.

Grammatical notes

1. Possession

In the above example, **bâan khun** บ้านคุณ means "your house," or more literally "house of you," so from this we can see that in Thai possession is indicated by word order: the possessor follows the thing possessed, without a word for "of" or an "apostrophe s."

However, in a more formal context we can say **bâan khǒrng khun** บ้านของคุณ, "your house," literally "house possession of you," so that this word **khǒrng** ของ can here be translated with "of."

2. Future

The word **jà'** จะ (observe the glottal stop at the end, like a *k*, but not written as such in Thai) indicates a future tense, such as "will, going to, want to… ." In the above examples, the English present continuous tense in the translations contains this future meaning.

13 MÊUA-RAI เมื่อไร when?

Khun jà' bpai mêua-rai? คุณจะไปเมื่อไร
When will you go?

→ **Phǒm jà' bpai wan níi.** ผมจะไปวันนี้
I'm going today.

→ **Chǎn jà' bpai phrûng níi.** ฉันจะไปพรุ่งนี้
I'm going tomorrow.

Khun maa thěung Grungthêhp mêua-rai?
คุณมาถึงกรุงเทพเมื่อไร
When did you arrive in Bangkok?

→ **Mêua waan níi.** เมื่อวานนี้ Yesterday.
→ **Athít thîi láew.** อาทิตย์ ที่แล้ว Last week.
→ **Wan Phút.** วันพุธ On Wednesday.

Mêua-rai khun jà maa? เมื่อไร คุณ จะมา
When will you come?

Note on word order

You can see above, and in the examples below, that the
question word ("when?", "why?", "how?", and so on)
does not always have to be placed first in the sentence,
as it does in English, but can come last just as well.

14 THAM-MAI ทำไม why?

Khun maa Chiangmai tham-mai?
คุณมาเชียงใหม่ทำไม
Why have you come to Chiangmai?

→ **Maa thîau.** มาเที่ยว
   On holiday (for leisure, recreation).
→ **Maa thurá'.** มาธุระ On business.

Tham-mai maa cháa? ทำไม มาช้า
Why did you come late?

→ **Rót dtìt.** รถติด There was a traffic jam.
→ **Fǒn dtòk mâak.** ฝนตกมาก There was heavy rain.
→ **Chǎn dtèun sǎai.** ฉันตื่นสาย I woke up late.

15 YANG-NGAI (informal); YANG-RAI (formal) how?

Khun maa thîi nîi yang-ngai? คุณ มา ที่นี่ ยังไง
How did you get here?

→ **Maa taxi.** มาแทกซี่ I came by taxi.

Phǒm jà' bpai Ayutthia yang-ngai?
ผมจะไปอยุธยายังไง   How do I get to Ayutthia?

→ **Bpai thaang reua.** ไปทางเรือ By boat.
→ **Bpai rót yon.** ไปรถยนต์ By car.

Gin yang-ngai? กินยังไง How do I eat it?

→ **Chái chórn.** ใช้ช้อน With a spoon.
→ **Chái dta-gìap.** ใช้ตะเกียบ With chopsticks.

Note

The word **chái** ใช้ is actually a verb, meaning "to use," but in some places can better be translated with "with, using."

16 KHRAI? ใคร who?

Khǎu bpen khrai? เขา เป็นใคร Who is she/he?

→ **Khǎu bpen phêuan.** เขาเป็นเพื่อน
She/he's a friend.

Khrai phûut khá? ใครพูดคะ
Who's speaking? (on the telephone) (*woman asking*)

→ **Sǒmmǎi phûut.** สมหมายพูด
This is Sommai (speaking).

Khrai bòrk khun? ใครบอกคุณ Who told you?

→ **Hǔa nâa bòrk.** หัวหน้าบอก The boss told me.

Khun bpai shopping gàp khrai?
คุณไปชอบปิ้งกับใคร
Who are you going shopping with?

→ **Bpai gàp Nók.** ไปกับนก I'm going with Nok.

Grammatical notes

1. The word **bpen** เป็น is used to say "to be" in the sense of "to occupy the position of." (It has other meanings as well.)
2. The polite words **khráp** ครับ and **khà** ค่ะ were mentioned above. Here, though, the word **khà** has got a high tone, **khá** คะ, because it comes at the end of a question. **Khráp** ครับ, on the other hand, never changes its tone.

17 THAANG NǍI ทางไหน

which way?
(which direction; which method?)

Bpai 7-Eleven thaang nǎi?
ไป เซเว่น อีเลเว่น ทางไหน
Which way to 7-Eleven?

Or:

rohng phayabaan โรงพยาบาล hospital

sathăanii dtamruat สถานี ตำรวจ a police station

sathăan thûut สถานทูต embassy

ATM เอทีเอ็ม automated teller machine

kli-nik คลีนิค clinic

hăa mŏr หาหมอ to consult a doctor

hăa mŏr fan หาหมอฟัน to consult a dentist

→ **Bpai thaang sáai.** ไปทางซ้าย Go to the left.
→ **Deun dtrong bpai.** เดินตรงไป Go straight ahead.
→ **Lîau khwăa.** เลี้ยวขวา Turn right.
→ **Bpai thaang níi.** ไปทางนี้ Go this way.
→ **Bpai thaang nán.** ไปทางนั้น Go that way.

Bpai Wát Pho thaang năi? ไปวัดโพธิ์ ทางไหน
How do I (you) get to Wat Pho?

→ **Bpai rót bas ber 56.** ไป รถบัส เบอร์ 56
  On bus number 56.

→ **Bpai rót taxi.** ไปรถแท็กซี่ By taxi.

Note also the useful term: **thaang òrk** ทางออก exit, way out.

18 THÂU-RAI? เท่าไร how much?

Níi thâu-rai? นี่เท่าไร How much is this?

An níi raakhaa thâu-rai? อันนี้ ราคา เท่าไร
How much does this cost? (literally "this item, price how much?")

Khun aayú' thâu-rai? คุณ อายุเท่าไร
How old are you?

→ **Chǎn aayú' hòk-sìp bpii.** ฉันอายุ 60 ปี
I'm (aged) sixty.

Naan thâu-rai? นาน เท่าไร
How long (will it take)?

→ **Bpra-maan sǒng chûa-mong.**
ประมาณ สอง ชั่ว โมง
Approximately two hours.

Jàak sanǎam-bin bpai rong-raem, gin wehlaa naan thâu-rai?

จากสนามบินไปโรงแรมกินเวลานานเท่าไร

How long does it take to get from the airport to the hotel?

→ **Rau-rau khrêung chûamong.**

ราว ราว ครึ่งชั่วโมง About half an hour.

19 GÌI? กี่ how many?

Gìi chûa-mong? กี่ ชั่วโมง How many hours?

Khun mii lûuk gìi khon? คุณมีลูกกี่คน

How many children do you have?

Gìi bàht? กี่บาท

How many baht (how much does it cost)?

→ **Róoi hâa-sìp bàht.** 150 บาท

One hundred and fifty baht.

Gìi wan? กี่วัน How many days?

Gìi deuan? กี่เดือน How many months?

Gìi bpii? กี่ปี How many years?

Grammatical note

We see the word **khon** คน (person, people) used as a counting word (also called a "numeral classifier") above, so we get literally "children how many people." Thai has a very extensive system of counting words, but the beginning student does not need to deal with more than a few of these. It is best to compare the situation with similar expressions in English, such as "head of cattle," or "pieces of information." For counting people, **khon** คน should be used. The word **an** อัน, which we met earlier, can also serve as a kind of neutral counting word, if you don't happen to know the right one, e.g. **gìi an**? กี่ อัน how many "things"?

20 GÔR DÂI ก็ได้
any- (please yourself)

Khun jà' gin arai? คุณจะกิน อะไร
What are you going to eat?

→ **Arai gôr dâi!** อะไร ก็ได้
  Anything! (Whatever you like, I don't mind)

Yùt thîi nǎi? หยุดที่ไหน Where will we stop?

→ **Thîi nǎi gôr dâi.** ที่ไหนก็ได้. Anywhere you like.

Mêua-rai òrk jàak hông níi? เมื่อไหร่ ออกจากห้องนี้
What time do we leave this room?

→ **Mêua-rai gôr dâi** เมื่อไหร่ก็ได้
   Any time (at your convenience).

Khrai jà' bpai séu ahǎan?
ใครจะไปซื้ออาหาร Who's going to buy the food?

→ **Khrai gôr dâi.** ใครก็ได้ Anybody (it doesn't matter).

Note
Here we see that the question words can also have an indefinite function. Something similar happens with a negative in some cases, e.g.:

Mâi bpen rai (rai = arai) ไม่เป็นไร
It's nothing (it doesn't matter, it's okay).

Mâi mii khrai yùu. ไม่มีใครอยู
There's no one there (here) (no one at home).

PART 3

Words 21–30

Ordering a meal

21 HĬU หิว hungry

Khun hĭu măi? คุณหิวไหม Are you hungry?

→ **Hĭu nít nòi.** หิวนิดหน่อย A bit hungry.
→ **Hĭu mâak.** หิวมาก Very hungry.
→ **Mâi hĭu.** ไม่หิว I'm not hungry.

Hĭu náam. หิวน้ำ I'm thirsty (literally "hungry for water").

Hĭu khâao. หิวข้าว
I want something to eat (literally "hungry for rice"—rice represents food in general, as it is the most important food).

22 YÀAK อยาก

want to, would like to…

Phǒm yàak gin ahǎan Thai. ผมอยากกินอาหารไทย
I would like to eat (some) Thai food.

Chǎn yàak bpai Siam Square.
ฉันอยากไปสยามสแควร
I would like to go to Siam Square.

Rau yàak gin thîi ráan rim.
เราอยากกินที่ร้านริมน้ำ
We would like to eat (have a meal) at a restaurant on
the edge of the river.

Khǎu yàak gin nai reua. เขาอยากกินในเรือ
He/she wants to eat on (Thai: in) the boat.

Phǒm mâi yàak gin bia. ผมไม่อยากกินเบียร์
I don't want to drink (Thai: "eat"!) beer.

23 KHǑR ขอ

may I have…? (polite request)

Khǒr menu. ขอเมนู May I have the menu?

Khŏr khâao nèung môr. ขอข้าว 1 หม้อ
May I have one pot of rice?

Khŏr gaeng sŏng thîi. ขอแกง 2 ที่
May I have two servings of curry? (literally "curry two places")

Khŏr náam săam gâeu. ขอน้ำ 3 แก้ว
May I have three glasses of water?

Khŏr Pepsi sìi khwàt. ขอเป็ปซี่ 4 ขวด
May I have four bottles of Pepsi?

Khŏr gaafae hâa thûay. ขอกาแฟ 5 ถ้วย
May I have five cups of coffee?

Also:

Khŏr thôot. ขอโทษ
I beg your pardon (excuse me, sorry).

24 AU เอา I want; bring me; I'll take…

Phŏm au dtôm yam gûng nèung thîi.
ผมเอาต้มยำกุ้ง 1 ที่
I want one serving of "tom yam gung" (spicy prawn soup).

Chăn au khâao phàt nèung jaan.

ฉันเอาข้าวผัด 1 จาน

I want a (one) plate of fried rice.

Khun au bia măi? คุณเอาเบียร์ไหม

Do you want beer?

→ **Mâi au!** ไม่เอา No, I don't.
   (Note repetition of the verb in this answer.)
→ **Au Pepsi.** เอาเป๊ปซี่ I'll have a Pepsi.

Khun au náam khĕng dûai măi?

คุณเอาน้ำแข็งด้วยไหม Will you have ice with that?

→ **Au dûai.** เอาด้วย Yes, I will.

Au náam chaa rĕu gaafae? เอาน้ำชาหรือกาแฟ

Will you have tea or coffee?

→ **Au náam chaa.** เอาน้ำชา I'll have tea.

Au ìik! เอาอีก I want another/more!

25 NÒI หน่อย

a little; a particle that softens a request, placed in final position

Khŏr gaafae rórn nòi. ขอกาแฟร้อนหน่อย
Could I have some hot coffee, please?

Khŏr náam nòi. ขอน้ำหน่อย
Could I have some water, please?

Sài nom nít nòi. ใส่นมนิดหน่อย
With a little milk in it.

Sài nám-dtaan nít nòi. ใส่น้ำตาลนิดหน่อย
With a little sugar in it.

Khŏr nám-dtaan ìik nòi. ขอน้ำตาลอีกหน่อย
Could I have a little more sugar, please?

Mâi sài nom. ไม่ใส่นม Without milk.

Mâi sài nám-dtaan. ไม่ใส่น้ำตาล Without sugar.

Note: the verb **sài** ใส่ has various meanings: "to put into; to include, insert; to wear (clothes)."

26 CHÔRP ชอบ

to like, have a liking for

Phŏm chôrp gaeng néua. ผมชอบแกงเนื้อ
I like beef curry.

Kău chôrp dtôm yam gûng mâak.
เขาชอบต้มยำกุ้งมาก
She likes "tom yam gung" soup very much.

Faràng mâi chôrp thurian, mĕn mâak.
ฝรั่งไม่ชอบทุเรียน, เหม็นมาก
Foreigners don't like durian—it's very smelly.

Chăn chôrp phèt. ฉัน ชอบ เผ็ด
I like it hot (hot food).

Chăn chôrp thúk yaang. ฉันชอบทุกอย่าง
I like any kind (of food).

Khun Manát chôrp bplaa mâak gwàa gài.
คุณ มนัส ชอบปลา มากกว่า ไก่
Mr Manat likes fish more than chicken.

Note: We use **gwàa** กว่า to say "more" (*-er*) when making a comparison, e.g. **dii gwàa** ดีกว่า, "better."

27 PHÈT เผ็ด hot (spicy)

Khun chôrp phèt măi? คุณชอบเผ็ดไหม
Do you like hot food?

→ **Chôrp phèt nít nòi.** ชอบเผ็ดนิดหน่อย
  I like it a bit hot.

→ **Chôrp phèt bpaan-glaang.** ชอบเผดปานกลาง
  I like it medium hot.

→ **Chôrp phèt mâak.** ชอบเผ็ดมาก I like it very hot.

→ **Mâi chôrp phèt leui.** ไม่ชอบเผ็ดเลย
  I don't like it hot at all.

Gaeng gài níi phèt mâak. แกงไก่นี้เผ็ดมาก
This chicken curry is very hot.

Gaeng bplaa mâi khôi phèt. แกงปลาไม่ค่อยเผ็ด
The fish curry isn't very hot.

Náam jîm phèt mâak-mâak! น้ำจิ้มเผ็ดมากมาก
The sauce (dip) is very, very hot!

28 ARÒI อร่อย delicious, tasty, nice

Ahăan Thai aròi măi? อาหารไทยอร่อยไหม
Is Thai food tasty?

→ **Aròi mâak!** อร่อยมาก It's very delicious!

Gaeng phèt gài, aròi măi? แกงเผ็ดไก่ อร่อยไหม
Is the spicy chicken curry tasty?

Gaeng mŭu aròi gwàa gaeng gài.
แกงหมู อร่อย กว่า แกงไก่
The pork curry is tastier than the chicken.

Gaeng néua aròi thîi-sùt. แกงเนื้อ อร่อยที่สุด
The beef curry is the tastiest (of all).

Note: we can say "the most" (-*est*) using the word
thîi-sùt ที่สุด placed after an adjective, as above.

29 **ÌM อิ่ม full; to have had enough**

Ìm măi? อิ่มไหม Have you had enough?

→ **Ìm láew** อิ่มแล้ว Yes, I have (literally "already
  full").
→ **Yang mâi ìm.** ยังไม่อิ่ม
  Not yet (I'd like some more).
→ **Ìm mâak!** อิ่มมาก I'm very full!

▣30 AHǍAN อาหาร

food, meal (Note: the spelling in Thai is **aahǎan**
อาหาร, but the first "a" is pronounced short.)

Ahǎan Thai. อาหารไทย Thai food.

Ahǎan cháau. อาหารเช้า Breakfast.

Ahǎan thîang. อาหารเที่ยง Lunch.

Ahǎan yen. อาหารเย็น Dinner.

Ahǎan khâm. อาหารค่ำ Supper.

Cultural note
Table etiquette in Thailand

Most visitors to Thailand look forward to enjoying
Thai food, which is justly famous for its delicious fla-
vors, produced with interesting sauces and herbs—not
just chillis! This food can be found in many good res-
taurants (**ráan ahǎan**) ร้านอาหาร and hotels, but do
be cautious about eating from the many roadside stalls,
as they may not be very clean, and the noise of the traffic in the street is a nuisance too.

Thai food is eaten with a spoon and fork, but
Chinese dishes such as noodles can better be eaten with
chopsticks, which take some practice to use. When

passing or receiving food, use your right hand, as the left is considered as less polite. It is also important not to reach over or stand over someone's head, as this is regarded as a space not to be intruded on.

The most senior (oldest) people present are served first, and the younger ones help them. Wait till the others have been served before beginning.

The rice is regarded as the main part of the meal. The other dishes are mere auxiliaries added to it, and so are termed **gàp-khâao** กับข้าว, literally "with the rice." Take your rice first, and then add other things to it. Do not dip your own spoon into the common dish if you are sharing it with the others.

It is best to take plain water (**nám bplàau** น้ำเปล่า) with your meal. The custom is to drink after you have finished eating, rather than during the meal. To relieve the burning taste of too many chillis, just take some more plain rice. Fruit may be served to finish up and freshen the mouth.

To call a waiter (more likely a waitress) (**khon serp** คนเสริพ, from English "serve"), just raise your hand. If you beckon, do it with the fingers down, not up. Thais will address the waiter with **nóng** น้อง ("younger brother/sister"), but foreigners may not feel comfortable with this.

Cheun khráp. เชิญครับ
Please go ahead (literally "I invite you").

PART 4

Words 31–40

Shopping and negotiating

31 SÉU ซื้อ to buy

Khun jà' séu arai? คุณจะซื้ออะไร
What do you want to buy?

Phŏm/chǎn jà' séu gang-gehng.
ผม ฉัน จะ ซื้อ กางเกง I want to buy pants.

Substitute the noun underlined:

sêua phûu yǐng	เสื้อผู้หญิง	a blouse
sêua yêut	เสื้อ ยืด	a T-shirt
gra-bprong	กระโปรง	a skirt
nek tai	เนคไท	a tie
phâa mǎi	ผ้าไหม	silk cloth
phâa fâai	ผ้าฝ้าย	cotton cloth
chút norn	ชุดนอน	pyjamas

Séu rorng-tháau thîi năi? ซื้อรองเท้าที่ไหน
Where do we buy shoes?

→ **Thîi dtalàat** ที่ตลาด In the market.
→ **Thîi depaatmen** ที่ ดีพาร์ท เม็น
   In a department store.
→ **Thîi supermarket** ที่ซุปเปอร์มาเก็ต
   In a supermarket.
→ **Thîi chán săam** ที่ชั้น สาม On the third floor.

Note: In Thailand there is no ground floor—the numbering starts with level 1.

32 RAA-KHAA ราคา price

Níi raa-khaa thâu-rai? นี่ราคาเท่าไหร่
What is the price of this?

Nán raa-khaa thâu-rai? นั่นราคาเท่าไหร่
What is the price of that?

→ **Raa-khaa róoi bàht.** ราคา 100 บาท
   It costs a hundred baht.
→ **Sŏng róoi bàht.** ราคา 200 บาท
   Two hundred baht.

→ **Raa-khaa thùuk.** ราคาถูก A cheap (low) price.
→ **Raa-khaa phaeng gern-bpai.** ราคาแพงเกินไป
  Too high a price (too expensive).
→ **Raa-khaa moksŏm.** ราคาเหมาะสม
  A reasonable (good) price.

33 LÓT ลด to reduce, lower

Lót raa-khaa dâi mâi? ลดราคาได้ไหม
Can you lower the price?

Lót ìik dâi mâi? ลดอีกได้ไห
Can you lower it a bit more?

→ **Lót mâi dâi.** ลดไม่ได้ I can't reduce it!
→ **Lót dâi nít nòi.** ลดได้นิดหน่อย
  I can reduce it a bit.
→ **Lót láew.** ลดแล้ว I've already reduced it!

Thîi supermarket lót mâi dâi.
ที่ซุปเปอร์มาเก็ต ลดไม่ได้
Prices can't be reduced in a supermarket.

Grammatical note
Note the word order: **lót raa-khaa mâi dâi**
ลดราคาไม่ได้, literally "reduce price not can." We can't
alter this order and put **mâi dâi** in front, for instance.

Cultural note

It is quite acceptable to bargain in any market in Thailand—the Thais expect it. One method is to halve the seller's starting price, and then come up half of the difference. The result should then be very reasonable. The prices charged to foreigners are always higher than for the locals, so if you can get some reduction you've done well. But don't try it in a supermarket or department store, of course.

34 KHANÀAT ขนาด size; SǏI สี color

Khanàat nǎi? ขนาดไหน Which size?

Note: **Nǎi** ไหน suggests a choice out of many possible ones; **arai** อะไร "what?" could not be used here.

→ **Khanàat lék.** ขนาด เล็ก Small (size).
→ **Khanàat glaang.** ขนาด กลาง Medium (size).
→ **Khanàat yài.** ขนาด ใหญ่ Large.
→ **Khanàat ber bàet.** ขนาด เบอร์ แปด
      Size (number) 8.

Sǐi arai? สีอะไร What color?

→ **Sǐi dam**   สีดำ   Black
→ **Sǐi daeng**   สีแดง   Red

→ **Sǐi khǎau**   สีขาว   White
→ **Sǐi khǐau**   สีเขียว   Green

Note: We repeat the word **sǐi** สี before specifying the color.

35 PHA-NÀEK แผนก
department, section

Pha-nàek sêua phâa. แผนกเสื้อผ้า
Clothing department.

Pha-nàek rohng táu. แผนกรองเท้า
Shoe department.

Pha-nàek grabpǎu. แผนกกระเป๋า Bag department.

Pha-nàek phâa yùu thîi nǎi? แผนกผ้าอยู่ที่ไหน
Where is the clothing department?

→ **Yùu chán sìi.** อยู่ชั้นสี่
On the fourth floor (literally "floor four").

36 KHǍAI ขาย to sell

Khǎai gài yâang. ขายไก่ย่าง We sell roast chicken.

Rau khăai komputêr. เราขายคอมพิวเตอร์
We sell computers.

Rau khăai bplìik. เราขายปลีก We sell retail.

Rau khăai sòng. เราขายส่ง We sell wholesale.

Khít raakhaa khăai sòng. คิดราคาขายส่ง
Charge (calculate) your wholesale price.

Khít raakhaa khon Thai. คิดราคาคนไทย
Charge the local price (for Thai people).

37 JÀAI จ่าย to pay

Phŏm jàai ngeun sòt. ผมจ่ายเงินสด I'll pay cash.

Chăn jàai dûai bàt kredit. ฉันจ่ายด้วยบัตรเครดิต
I'll pay by (with) credit card.

Rau jàai dûai chék. เราจ่ายด้วยเช็ค
We'll pay by cheque.

Khău jàai khròp/ tháng-mòt. เขาจ่ายครบทั้งหมด
He pays (it) off completely.

→ **Jàai thii dîau.** จ่าย ทีเดียว In one go.

→ **Jàai phon sòng.** จ่าย ผ่อนส่ง In installments.

→ **Jàai athit lá'nèung róoi bàht.**
  จ่าย อาทิตย์ ละ ร้อยบาท
  100 baht per week (weekly).

→ **Jàai deuan lá' sìi róoi bàht.**
  จ่าย เดือน ละ สี่ ร้อย บาท
  400 baht per month (monthly).

→ **Jàai bpii lá' hâa phan bàht.**
  จ่าย ปี ละ ห้า พัน บาท
  5,000 baht per year (annually).

On the numerals, refer to pages 65 – 68.

38 CHÂU เช่า to rent, hire

Châu <u>rót</u>. เช่ารถ To rent a car.

Substitute the noun underlined:
modtersai มอเตอร์ไซ a motorcycle
bâan บ้าน a house
apartmen อพาร์ตเม็นท์ an apartment
kondo คอนโด; **hohng-chut** ห้องชุด a condominium

Châu rót raa-khaa thâu-rai? เช่ารถราคาเท่าไร
How much does it cost to rent a car?

→ **Athít lá' hâa róoi bàht.** อาทิตย์ละห้าร้อยบาท
500 baht per week.

→ **Deuan lá' sŏng phan bàht.** เดือนละสองพันบาท
2,000 baht per month.

→ **Mèun sŏng phan bàht dtòr hòk deuan.**
หมื่นสองพันบาทต่อหกเดือน
12,000 baht for six months.

Compare also **mǎu rót** เหมารถ, to charter a car (e.g. for group travel up-country), **bpai glàp** ไปกลับ, out and back (return).

39 KHÂA ค่า fare, rate, tariff

Khâa châu. ค่าเช่า Rental rate

Khâa châu bâan thâu-rai? ค่าเช่าบ้านเท่าไร
How much is the rental of the house?

Khâa châu rót thâu-rai? ค่าเช่ารถเท่าไร
How much is the rental for a car?

Khâa taxi thâu-rai? ค่าแท็กซี่เท่าไร
How much is the taxi fare?

40 LÂEK แลก to exchange (money)

Lâek ngeun. แลกเงิน To exchange money.

Lâek chék. แลกเช็ค
To exchange a (traveler's) check.

Lâek dollar bpen ngeun bàht.
แลก ดอลลาร์ เป็น เงิน บาท
To exchange dollars for baht.

(Note the use of **bpen** เป็น "be, become" here.)

Khŏr lâek bai lá' róoi. ขอแลกใบละร้อย
Could I please have notes (bills) of one hundred?

Khŏr lâek hâa róoi bàht sŏng bai.
ขอแลก ห้าร้อยบาท สองใบ
May I have two notes of 500 baht?

Khŏr lâek nèung phan dollar.
ขอแลก หนึ่งพันดอลล่าร์
Could you change 1,000 dollars?

Au bank róoi bàht. เอาแบ็งค์ ร้อย บาท
I want notes of 100 baht.

Notes

1. The Thai for "banknote" is just **bank** แบ็งค์. The counting word for banknotes is **bai** ใบ "leaf."

2. There is a different word for "change" (money given back after a transaction), namely **ngeun thorn** เงินทอน (pronounced "torn").

Useful phrases relating to money:

Khŏr ngeun thorn. ขอเงินทอน
May I have my change?

Ngeun thorn thâu-rai? เงินทอนเท่าไร
How much is the change?

Mâi dtông thorn. ไม่ต้องทอน
No need to give change (keep the change).

Phŏm hâi thíp khun. ผมให้ทิปคุณ
It's a tip for you.

Numerals

The system of numerals is quite regular, but has some unexpected terms. It works as follows:

1	**nèung**	หนึ่ง
2	**sŏng**	สอง
3	**săam**	สาม

4	**sìi**	สี่
5	**hâa**	ห้า
6	**hòk**	หก
7	**jèt**	เจ็ด
8	**bàet**	แปด
9	**gâau**	เก้า
10	**sìp**	สิบ
11	**sìp-èt**	สิบเอ็ด
12	**sìp-sŏng**	สิบสอง
13	**sìp-săam**	สิบสาม
14	**sìp-sìi**	สิบสี่
15	**sìp-hâa**	สิบห้า
16	**sìp-hòk**	สิบหก
17	**sìp-jèt**	สิบเจ็ด
18	**sìp-bàet**	สิบแปด
19	**sìp-gâau**	สิบเก้า
20	**yîi-sìp**	ยี่สิบ
	[not "**sŏng-sìp**"!]	
21	**yîi-sìp-èt**	ยี่ สิบ เอ็ด
22	**yîi-sìp-sŏng**	ยี่สิบสอง
23	**yîi-sìp-săam**	ยี่สิบสาม
30	**săam-sìp**	สามสิบ
40	**sìi-sìp**	สี่สิบ
50	**hâa-sìp**	ห้าสิบ
60	**hòk-sìp**	หกสิบ
70	**jèt-sìp**	เจ็ดสิบ

80	**bàet-sìp**	แปดสิบ
90	**gâau-sìp**	เก้าสิบ
100	**róoi**	หนึ่งร้อย or ร้อย
200	**sŏng róoi**	สองร้อย
300	**săam róoi**	สามร้อย
400	**sìi róoi**	สี่ร้อย
500	**hâa róoi**	ห้าร้อย
600	**hòk róoi**	หก ร้อย
700	**jèt róoi**	เจ็ดร้อย
800	**bàet róoi**	แปดร้อย
900	**gâau róoi**	เก้าร้อย
1,000	**phan**	หนึ่งพัน or พัน
2,000	**sŏng phan**	สอง พัน
3,000	**săam phan**	สาม พัน etc.,

but

10,000	**mèun**	หนึ่งหมื่น or หมื่น
20,000	**sŏng mèun**	สองหมื่น etc.
100,000	**săen**	แสน
300,000	**săam săen**	สามแสน etc.
1,000,000	**láan**	หนึ่งล้าน or ล้าน
4,000,000	**sìi láan**	สี่ล้าน etc.

It is important to memorize these large units, as they do not follow the Western system of "ten thousand" or "one hundred thousand."

In order to make an ordinal number, we just use the word **thîi** ที่ in front of the cardinal number, e.g. **thîi hâa** ที่ ห้า, "fifth."

PART 5

Words 41–50

Getting about

41 **DÛAI** with, by means of **ด้วย**

Phŏm jà' bpai Hŭa-hĭn yang-ngai?
ผมจะไปหัวหิน ยังไง How do I get to Hua-hin?

Chăn jà' bpai Chiangmai yàng-rai?
ฉันจะไปเชียงใหม่อย่างไร
How do I get to Chiangmai?

→ **Bpai dûai reua.** ไปด้วยเรือ By boat.
→ **Bpai dûai rót bas.** ไปด้วยรถบัส By bus.
→ **Bpai dûai rót fai.** ไปด้วย รถไฟ By train.
→ **Bpai dûai khrêuang bin.** ไปด้วยเครื่องบิน
   By plane.
→ **Bpai dûai rót fai fáa.** ไปด้วยรถไฟฟ้า
   By skytrain.

42 **KHÊUN** ขึ้น

to go up, ascend; to get on (a mode of transport); to increase, get more

Khêun rót fai thîi năi? ขึ้นรถไฟที่ไหน
Where do you get on the train?

→ **Thîi Hŭa-lampong.** ที่หัวลำโพง
   At Hualampong (Bangkok's main station)
→ **Thîi sathăanii rót fai.** ที่สถานีรถไฟ
   At the station.

Khêun bandai. ขึ้นบันได To go up the stairs.

Khêun chán bon. ขึ้นชั้นบน
To go (up) to the upper level.

Khêun chán bon-sùt. ขึ้น ชั้น บนสุด
To go to the very top.

Khêun líp bpai chán sìp. ขึ้น ลิฟท์ ไป ชั้น สิบ
To take the lift to level 10.

Dii khêun. ดีขึ้น To get (become) better.

Tham hâi piŭ khăau khêun. ทำ ให้ ผิว ขาว ขึ้น
It gives you whiter skin.

(Note the word order in these last two examples.)

43 LONG ลง
to go down; to get off (a mode of transport)

Phǒm long rót thîi Siam Square.
ผม ลงรถ ที่ สยามแสควร
I get (got) off the bus at Siam Square.

Chǎn long rót fai thîi sathǎanii Sǎmsěn.
ฉันลงรถไฟที่สถานีสามเสน
I get (got) off the train at Samsen Station.

Rau long rót bas thîi sathǎn thûut Australia.
เราลงรถบัสที่สถานทูต ออสเตรเลีย
We get off the bus at the Australian embassy.

Khǎu long rót taxi thîi Sǔansàt Dusit.
เขาลงรถแท็กซี่ที่สวนสัตว์ดุสิต
He got out of the taxi at Dusit Zoo.

Khǎu long khrêuang bin thîi Phuket.
เขาลงเครื่องบินที่ภูเก็ต
She got off the plane in Phuket.

BUT

Chăn long reua thîi Thammasat.

ฉันลงเรือที่ธรรมศาสตร์

I got on the boat at Thammasat.

Note: This is an exception—you have to step down to get on the boat. And to get off you have to **khêun fàng** ขึ้นฝั่ง, "climb the bank"!

44 JORNG จอง to book, reserve

Phŏm jorng thîi nâng săam thîi. ผมจองที่นั่งสามที่

I booked three seats.

Chăn jorng dtŭa săam thîi. ฉันจองตั๋ว สามที่

I reserved three tickets.

Note: In these two examples, the word **thîi** ที่ ("place") serves as a counting word for seats or tickets. These could be on a bus, train, plane or even in a restaurant or at a seminar.

Rau jà' jorng hông nèung hông.

เราจะจองห้องหนึ่งห้อง We want to book one room.

Note: Again, the second **hông** ห้อง is a counting word. The room could be:

Hông dîau ห้องเดี่ยว a single room, or
Hông khûu ห้องคู่ a double room (room for two),

or you could say

Dtiang dîau เตียงเดี่ยว a single bed, or
Dtiang khûu เตียงคู่ a double bed.

45 GLAI ไกล far; GLÂI ไกล้ close

Because these two words have opposite meanings and only a different tone to distinguish them in pronunciation, they are listed together here. Note the word order in the examples below.

Jàak Grungthêhp bpai Ayutthia glai măi?
จาก กรุงเทพ ไป อยุธยา ไกลไหม
Is it far from Bangkok to Ayutthia?

→ **Glai mâak.** ไกล มาก It's a long way.

Glai mâak khâe- năi? ไกล มาก แค่ ไหน How far?

Glai gìi giloh? ไกล กี่ กิโล How many kilometers?

→ **Rau-rau róoi giloh.** ราว ราว ร้อย กิโล
About a hundred kilometers.

Jàak Grungthêhp bpai Phuket glai măi?
จากกรุงเทพไปภูเก็ต ไกลไหม
It is far from Bangkok to Phuket?

→ **Glai mâak.** ไกลมาก It's a very long way.

Gìi giloh? กี่ กิโล How many kilometers?

→ **Mâi rúu.** ไม่รู้ I don't know;
mâi sâap ไม่ทราบ (more polite)

Jàak thîi nîi bpai 7-Eleven glai măi? จากที่นี่ไปเซเว่
นอีเล็บเว่น ไกลไหม Is it far from here to 7-Eleven?

→ **Glâi.** ใกล้ It's close.
→ **Glâi mâak.** ใกล้มาก It's very close.
→ **Deun bpai dâi.** เดินไปได้ You can walk.
→ **Deun sìp-hâa nathii.** เดิน สิบห้านาที
It's 15 minutes' walk.
→ **Khêun rót hâa nathii.** ขึ้นรถ ห้านาที
It's 5 minutes by car.

46 THANŎN ถนน road; SOI ซอย side-street

Sathăan-thûut Australia yùu thîi năi?
สถานทูต ออสเตรเลีย อยู่ที่ไหน
Where is the Australian embassy?

Thîi thanŏn arai? ที่ถนนอะไร On which road?

→ **Thîi thanŏn Sathorn dtâi.** ที่ ถนน สาทร ใต้
   On South Sathorn Road.

Rong-raem Mandarin yùu thîi năi?
โรงแรม แมนดาริน อยู่ ที่ ไหน
Where is the Mandarin Hotel?

→ **Thîi thanŏn Phra Ram 4.**
   ที่ ถนน พระ ราม สี่
   On Rama Road 4.

Note: The term **thanŏn** ถนน normally refers to a main road. On each side of a main city road (which may be very long) we have numbered side-streets, odd on one side and even on the other, called **soi**. So when looking for an address it's important to note which **soi** ซอย, and the house number within it. House numbers often have a slash (**tháp** ทับ), e.g. 334/5.

Khâam thanŏn. ข้ามถนน To cross the road.

Deun dtaam thanŏn. เดิน ตาม ถนน
To follow the road.

Glaang thanŏn. กลางถนน The middle of the road.

᠘ KHÂNG ข้าง side

khâng nâa ข้างหน้า the front

khâng lăng ข้างหลัง the back

khâng bon ข้างบน upstairs

khâng lâng ข้างหลัง downstairs

BUT for left and right

thaang sáai ทางซ้าย (on the) left-hand side

thaang kwăa ทางขวา (on the) right-hand side.

48 JANGWÀT จังหวัด

province (a common spelling is **Changwat**)

Bpai dtàang jangwàt. ไป ต่างจังหวัด
To go up-country (into the provinces, away from the capital)

Jangwàt Grabii [Krabii] mii chaihàat sǔay mâak.
จังหวัด กระบี่ มี ชายหาด สวย มาก
Krabii Province has very beautiful beaches.

Jangwàt Surin mii cháang maak.
จังหวัดสุรินทร์มีช้างมาก
Surin Province has lots of elephants.

Jangwàt Chiangrai mii phukhǎu sǔung.
จังหวัดเชียงรายมีภูเขาสูง
Chiangrai Province has high mountains.

Jangwàt Chiangmai mii aagàat dii.
จังหวัด เชียงใหม่ มี อากาศ ดี
Chiangmai Province has a good climate.

Note: A province is divided into districts, termed **ampheu** อำเภอ (also spelled **amphur**) and sub-districts termed **dtambon** ตำบล (or **tambon**). Below these is the lowest level—the village, **mùu-bâan** หมู่บ้าน.

49 SABAI สบาย comfortable, healthy

Nâng sabai măi? นั่งสบายใหม
Are you sitting comfortably?

Mêua kheun láp sabai măi? เมื่อคืนหลับสบายใหม
Did you have a good sleep last night?

→ **Sabai.** สบาย Yes, I did.
→ **Mâi khôi láp.** ไม่ค่อยหลับ I didn't sleep much.
→ **Láp-láp dtèun-dtèun.** หลับ หลับ ตื่น ตื่น
   I kept waking up.

Sabai dii. สบายดี In good health.

Phŏm mâi sabai. ผมไม่สบาย I'm not feeling well.

Phŏm mâi khôi sabai. ผมไม่ค่อยสบาย
I'm not very well.

Sabai jai. สบายใจ
Happy, contented (literally "comfortable at heart.")

50 THĔUNG ถึง to reach, arrive at

Bpai thĕung Phuket dton-năi?
ไปถึงภูเก็ต ตอนใหน When do we get to Phuket?

Chái wehlaa deun thaang sŏng chûamong.

ใช้เวลา เดินทาง 2 ชั่วโมง

It takes two hours to get there.

Rau maa thĕung bâan wan Jan.

เรามาถึงบ้าน วันจันทร์ We arrive home on Monday.

Bpai thĕung dtrong wehlaa. ไปถึงตรงเวลา

To arrive on time.

Bpai thĕung sǎi. ไปถึงสาย To arrive late.

Bpai thĕung cháa. ไปถึงช้า

To arrive late (behind time).

Khít thĕung. คิดถึง

To miss, be thinking of someone from afar.

PART 6

Words 51–60

Family and friends

▪51 PHÔR พ่อ father

Khun phôr tham ngaan thîi opfít.
คุณพ่อทำงานที่ อ๊อบฟิต
Father is working at the office.

Khun phôr ayú' thâu-rai? คุณพ่ออายุเท่าๆไร
How old is (your) father?

→ **Khun phôr ayú' hâa-sìp bpii.**
คุณพ่ออายุ 50 ปี Father is fifty years old.

Khun mâe yùu thîi nǎi? คุณแม่อยู่ที่ไหน
Where does your mother live?

→ **Thîi Isǎan, jangwàt Khon-gaen.**
ที่อีสาน จังหวัดขอนแก่น
In the North-East, Khon-gaen Province.

Notes

1. The title **khun** คุณ is put before kinship terms, as here, to indicate respect, either for one's own father or someone else's. The same applies to mother, uncle or aunt. The translation "Mr" or "Mrs" clearly does not apply.

2. **Isăan** อีสาน is one of the six regions of Thailand. The name means "north-east." These regions, termed **phâak** ภาค, are not official divisions, however, as is the case with the province.

Other terms:

Phôr dtaa: พ่อตา father-in-law (wife's father)

Phôr phǔa: พ่อผัว father-in-law (husband's father);
Phôr săamii: พ่อสามี (more formal/polite)

Phôr bâan: พ่อบ้าน head of the household

Phôr líang: พ่อเลี้ยง step-father.

52 MÂE แม่ mother

Khun mâe tham ahăan nai khrua.
คุณแม่ทำอาหารในครัว
Mother is cooking in the kitchen.

Mâe au khayá' bpai thíng. แม่เอาขยะไปทิ้ง
Mother takes the rubbish out (to throw away).

Mâe bâan sák phâa. แม่บ้านซักผ้า
The housekeeper is washing clothes.

Mâe phŭa: แม่ผัว mother-in-law (husband's mother)

Mâe yaai: แม่ยาย mother-in-law (wife's mother)

Mâe líang: แม่เลี้ยง step-mother

PHÔR-MÂE พ่อแม่ parents (father and mother)

Phôr-mâe rák lûuk. พ่อแม่รักลูก
Parents love their children.

Phôr-mâe mii lûuk sŏng khon. พ่อแม่มีลูกสองคน
My parents have two children.

Phôr-mâe sĭa chiiwít láew. พ่อแม่เสียชีวิตแล้ว
My parents are deceased (have passed away).

Note: The expression **sĭa chiiwít** เสียชีวิต (literally "to lose one's life") is respectful or formal; contrast plain **dtai** ตาย, to die.

53 PHÎI พี่

older sibling (brother or sister); **NÓNG**
น้อง younger sibling (brother or sister)

Phîi-nóng พี่ น้อง brothers and sisters (collectively)

Other terms:

Phîi khĕui: พี่ เขย
brother-in-law (husband of older sister)

Nóng khĕui: น้อง เขย
brother-in-law (husband of younger sister)

Phîi saphái: พี่สะใภ้
sister-in-law (wife of older brother)

Nóng saphái: น้องสะใภ้
sister-in-law (wife of younger brother)

Phîi líang: พี่เลี้ยง nurse (maid).

Cultural note

Thai society seems to take more interest in the relations
between people than a Western one does. This applies
in particular to the relationships within the family, but

the idea of "family" is extended beyond one's own real, blood, relatives to include others one comes into contact with. This is why people who are actually not related can address each other as **phîi** พี่ (elder brother/sister) or **nóng** น้อง (younger brother/sister), depending on their age. In this way everybody gets fitted into a framework of status and, consequently, of mutual obligations. In the "family" hierarchy, the younger members have to listen to and accept the judgments of the older ones. This can have benefits in terms of assistance and protection, but it also involves a degree of frustration and resentment in the face of tyranny from above.

So age difference is built into the terms for siblings, but not gender—the same terms apply to male and female siblings.

For more kinship terms, refer to the Appendix.

54 MIA เมีย wife (informal); PHANRAYAA ภรรยา wife (formal)

Phŏm phaa mia bpai hăa mŏr. ผมพาเมียไปหาหมอ
I took my wife to see a doctor.

Mia mii thórng. เมียมีท้อง She is pregnant.

Mia nói: เมียน้อย

a junior wife (unofficial, second wife; mistress).

55 PHǓA ผัว
husband (informal, impolite);
SǍAMII husband (formal)

Sǎamii khǒng chǎn bpen khon dii.
สามี ของ ฉัน เป็น คน ดี
My husband is a good person.

Sǎamii tham ngaan nàk. สามี ทำงานหนัก
My husband works hard.

Phǔa khîi-mao, mâi dii. ผัว ขี้เมา ไม่ ดี
A drunkard husband is not good.

Grammatical note

The Thai noun is neutral with regard to number, so **dèk**
เด็ก means both "child" and "children," but we can
double the word too, in order to make it clear that there
are more than one, and also to give the sentence a more
balanced sound.

56 **PHÊUAN** เพื่อน friend, companion

Rau bpen phêuan gan. เราเป็นเพื่อนกัน
We are friends.

Rau rák phêuan. เรารักเพื่อน We love our friends.

Khǎu mii phêuan mâak. เขา มี เพื่อน มาก
He/she has many friends.

Terms:
Phêuan khûu-jai. เพื่อนคู่ใจ a trusted friend

Phêuan bâan. เพื่อนบ้าน a neighbor

Phêuan chaai. เพื่อนชาย a male friend

Phêuan yǐng. เพื่อนหญิง a female friend.

BUT

faen แฟน girlfriend/boyfriend (from English "fan,"
admirer!)

57 **DTÀENG** means to decorate, as in:

dtàeng bâan แต่งบ้าน to decorate the house
dtàeng dtua แต่งตัว to get dressed
dtàeng nâa แต่งหน้า to put on make-up
dtàeng-ngaan แต่งงาน to get married

Khun dtàeng bâan dii. คุณ แต่งบ้าน ดี
You have decorated your house nicely.

Khun dtàeng dtua riap-róoi. คุณ แต่งตัว เรียบร้อย
You are dressed neatly.

Khun dtàeng nâa sǔai mâak. คุณแต่งหน้า สวยมาก
You are very nicely made up.

Khun dtàeng-ngaan rěu yang? คุแต่งงานหรือยัง
Are you married (or not yet)?
(Note: **rěu** หรือ, "or," is often pronounced **lěu**). To
answer this question, you could say:

➙ **bpen sòht.** เป็นโสด
I am unmarried (live a single life).
➙ **yâek-gan yùu gàp sǎamii.** แยก กัน อยู่ กับ สามี
I am separated from my husband.
➙ **yàa láew.** หย่าแล้ว I am divorced.
➙ **bpen mâe-mâai.** เป็นแม่หม้าย I am a widow.
➙ **bpen phôr-mâai.** เป็นพ่อหม้าย I am a widower.

Cultural note

Going to visit a friend

When visiting a friend, don't forget that you will have to take off your shoes before entering the house or apartment. This rule applies to anyone's home, but not a public building, unless a sign tells you otherwise: **garunaa thòrt rohng-tháau** กรุณาถอดรองเท้า, "kindly remove your shoes."

Thai people enjoy sitting around on the floor (on mats), even to enjoy a meal. In this case, be careful not to point your feet at other people, as this is considered extremely rude.

You should not stand over someone else's head, and if you have to pass something over their shoulder, say **Khǒr thôot** ขอโทษ, "Excuse me."

It is not necessary to bring a present, but a contribution to the food or drink would of course be appreciated.

58 KHON คน person, people

Khun bpen khon châat arai? คุณเป็นคนชาติอะไร
What is your nationality?

→ **Khǎu bpen khon Amerigan.** เขาเป็นคนอเมริกัน
He's an American.

(Note: the place is **Amerigaa** อเมริกา; and the adjective is **Amerigan**.)

Khǎu bpen khon Jiin. เขาเป็นคนจีน He's Chinese.
Yîi-bpùn ญี่ปุ่น Japanese.
Yeraman เยอรมัน German.
Faràngsèt ฝรั่งเศษ French.
Anggrìt อังกฤษ British.
("English" covers the whole of Britain!)

Note: The same adjectives for nationality generally apply to the language, e.g.:

Phaasǎa Jiin ภาษาจีน Chinese (language)
Yîi-bpùn ญี่ปุ่น Japanese
Faràngsèt ฝรั่ง เศษ French
Thai ไทย Thai
Anggrìt อังกฤษ English

59 JAI ใจ heart, mind

Khǎu bpen khon yang-ngai? เขาเป็นคนยังไง
What sort of person is he/she?

→ **Khǎu bpen khon jai-dii.** เขาเป็นคนใจดี
He is a kindhearted (good-natured) person.

There are many interesting expressions containing the word **jai** ใจ, some useful for understanding Thai values. Here is a selection (there are nouns, verbs and adjectives):

Grengjai: เกรงใจ
consideration; to be reluctant to impose on others

Glai dtaa, glai jai: ไกลตา ไกลใจ
out of sight, out of mind

Khòrp-jai! ขอบใจ Thanks!

Khâu-jai: เข้าใจ to understand

Bplìan jai: เปลี่ยนใจ to change one's mind

Jing-jai: จริงใจ sincere, heartfelt

Jai-dam: ใจดำ mean, selfish

Jèp-jai: เจ็บใจ hurt, offended

Jai-ngâai: ใจง่าย cheap, easy to get (woman)

Jai-dtên: ใจเต้น excited, with pounding heart

Jai-yen: ใจเย็น calm, cool-headed

Jai-sĭa: ใจเสีย disheartened; to lose heart

Cheun-jai: ชื่นใจ pleased, delighted, elated

Nám-jai: น้ำใจ thoughtfulness, goodwill

Sŏn-jai: สนใจ interested, absorbed (in)

Wăan-jai: หวานใจ sweetheart

Hŭa-jai: หัวใจ the heart (anatomical).

60 SĬA เสีย to spoil

Sĭa nâa เสียหน้า to lose face

Khun Chris mâi maa dtàeng-ngaan, tham-hâi Nók sĭa nâa.
คุณคริสไม่มาแต่งงาน ทำให้นกเสียหน้า
Chris didn't turn up for the wedding, so he made Nok lose face.

Ahăan sĭa léaw, yàa gin. อาหารเสียแล้วอย่ากิน
The food has gone bad, don't eat it.

Sĭa wehlaa sŏng chûa-mong phró' wâ rót dtìt.

เสียเวลา สองชั่วโมงเพราะว่ารถติด

I wasted two hours because of the traffic jam.

Sĭa rúu เสียรู้ to get tricked (for example, the taxi driver charges you double the rate promised).

PART 7

Words 61–70

Entertainments

61 THÎAU เที่ยว
trip, excursion, traveling about

Bpai thîau ไปเที่ยว
to go around (for pleasure), to go out (e.g. for the evening)

Thîi thîau ที่เที่ยว a place to go, to tour around

Maa thîau มาเที่ยว to come around (to someone's house, for a visit)

Bpai thîau glaang kheun ไปเที่ยวกลางคืน
to go out late at night

Bpai thîau gan theu'… . ไป เที่ยว กันเถอะ
Let's go out together.

62 DUU ดู to watch, look at

Duu thiiwii thîi bâan ดูทีวีที่บ้าน
to watch TV at home

Bpai duu năng ไปดูหนัง
to go and see a movie/film (**Note**: the Thai word **fiim** ฟิม refers only to photographic film.)

Duu show ดูโชว์ to watch a show
→ **Mii show lăai yàang.** มีโชว์หลายอย่าง
   There are shows of many kinds.
→ **Mii show dtorn dtèuk.** มีโชว์ตอนดึก
   There are late-night shows.

Duu lakhorn ดูละคร to watch a play/drama

Duu gilaa ดูกีฬา to watch sport/a game

Khâa duu ค่าดู admission fee

Duu thùuk ดูถูก to look down on, insult

63 SADĂENG แสดง
to perform, show, exhibit

Gaan sadăeng: การแสดง a performance, exhibition.

Grammatical note

The word **gaan** การ, placed in front of a verb, turns it into a noun, with the meaning of "the act of ...-ing."

Phûu sadăeng: ผู้แสดง player, performer

Raai chêu phûu sadăeng: รายชื่อผู้แสดง
cast, list of names of the performers/actors

Sadăeng lakhorn: แสดงละคร
to put on a play/drama

64 RÊUANG เรื่อง story, subject, matter

Năng rêuang arai? หนังเรื่องอะไร
What is the movie about? What is the title of the movie?

→ **Suriyothai.** สุริโยไทย
(the title of a famous movie about a queen from Thai history)

Prachum rêuang arai? ประชุมเรื่องอะไร
What is the meeting about?

→ **Rêuang ngaan Wan Dèk.** เรื่องงานวันเด็ก
It's about the celebration of Children's Day.

Mâi bpen rêuang ไม่เป็นเรื่อง to be nonsensical

Mâi rúu rêuang ไม่รู้เรื่อง
to have no understanding of the matter

65 **LÊN** เล่น
   to play; to do something for fun/amuse–
   ment, not seriously

Deun lên. เดินเล่น to go for a stroll

Gin lên. กินเล่น to have a snack

Phûut lên. พูดเล่น to joke around, tease

Norn lên. นอนเล่น to have a snooze

Lên gilaa. เล่นกีฬา to play sport/a game

Lên fútbon. เล่นฟุตบอล
to play football (that is, soccer, not other kinds)

Lên dondtrii. เล่นดนตรี to play music

Lên gii-dtâa. เล่นกีต้าร์ to play the guitar

66 **RÓRNG** ร้อง to cry out, utter a sound

Rórng plehng ร้องเพลง to sing a song

Rórng hái. ร้องให้ to cry, weep

Nák rórng นักร้อง a singer

Note: The word **nák** นัก, when placed in front of a verb, functions to make a noun with the meaning of "expert." Other examples are:

Nák-gilaa: นักกีฬา sportsman/woman, athlete

Nák-dtên ram: นัก เต้น รำ dancer

Nák-muay: นักมวย boxer

Nák-thuragìt: นักธุรกิจ businessman

Nak-thong-thîau: นักท่องเที่ยว traveler

67 **DTÊN RAM** เต้นรำ
to dance (ballroom)

Ram Thai รำไทย classical Thai dance

Ram wong รำวง

folk dance (couples moving in a circle)

Ram séung รำเซิ้ง

name of a folk dance from the North-East.

Mii dtên ago-go thîi night-club.
มีเต้นอะโกโก้ที่ไนท์คลับ

There is ago-go dancing in the night club.

Phŏm chôrp dtên ram. ผมชอบเต้นรำ

I like dancing.

Phŏm dtên ram mâi bpen. ผมเต้นรำไม่เป็น

I can't dance.

(Note that **bpen** here means "to be able," in the sense of having a particular skill.)

Khun dtên ram gàp phŏm măi?
คุณเต้นรำกับผมไหม

Will you dance with me?

68 **PLEHNG** เพลง song

Rórng plehng ร้องเพลง to sing a song

Dtàeng plehng แต่งเพลง to compose a song

Nák dtàeng plehng นักแต่งเพลง
a song writer, composer

Thamnorng plehng ทำนองเพลง melody, tune

Néua plehng เนื้อเพลง lyrics

Plehng châat เพลงชาติ the national anthem

69 DON-DTRII ดนตรี music

Don-dtrii Thai mii lǎai yàang. ดนตรีไทยมีหลายอย่าง
There are various sorts of Thai music:

Don-dtrii Thai deum: ดนตรีไทยเดิม
classical Thai music

Don-dtrii Thai saagon: ดนตรีไทยสากล
modern Thai music

Don-dtrii faràng: ดนตรีฝรั่ง Western music

Don-dtrii pheun-meuang: ดนตรีพื้นเมือง
regional music

70 SANÙK สนุก

   1) to have fun, enjoy oneself;
   2) to be fun, amusing, entertaining

Khwaam sanùk ความสนุก
amusement, fun, a good time

Grammatical note

The word **khwaam** ความ, placed in front of a verb or adjective, turns it into a noun with the abstract meaning of expressing a quality or state. Other examples are:

From **rúu** รู้, **khwaam rúu:** ความ รู้ knowledge

From **dii** ดี, **khwaam dii:** ความดี goodness

Nâa-sanùk: น่าสนุก to be fun, enjoyable

Sanùk dii: สนุกดี to be good fun; to have a good time

PART 8

Words 71–80

Telling and talking

71 WÂA ว่า that

Grammatical note

This word comes after verbs used for saying, asking, knowing and so on, and can be translated with "that" or "whether" (asking), or nothing, where it introduces a clause. For examples, see the following.

72 BÒRK บอก to say, tell, inform

Khun Tony bòrk wâa, khǎu chôrp bia Cháang.
คุณ โทนี่ บอก ว่า เขา ชอบ เบียร์ ช้าง
Tony said that he likes Elephant beer.

Khǎu bòrk wâa, mii mia láew.
เขาบอกว่ามีเมียแล้ว He said he already had a wife.

Chăn bòrk Mali wâa, yàa gèp ngeun thîi bon dtók.

ฉันบอกมะลิว่า อย่าเก็บเงินที่บนโต๊ะ

I told Mali not to (don't) take the money on the table.

Bòrk mâi thùuk. บอกไม่ถูก It's hard to say exactly.

73 PHÛUT พูด to speak, talk, say

Phûut phaasăa Anggrìt dâi mâi?

พูด ภาษา อังกฤษ ได้ ไหม Can you speak English?

→ **Phûut dâi nít nòi.** พูดได้นิดหน่อย

 I can speak it a bit.

Note the word order with **dâi** ได้ here.

→ **Phûut cháa-cháa nòi, (khráp/kà).**

 พูดช้าๆหน่อย (ครับ/ค่ะ) Please speak slowly.

Khău phûut gèng. เขาพูดเก่ง

He/she's good at speaking (it).

Note: The word **gèng** เก่ง, "skilled, good at something," is placed after the verb it refers to.

Khŏr phûut rêuang lûuk săau nòi.

ขอพูดเรื่องลูกสาวหน่อย

I would like to talk to you about your daughter.

Chau bâan phûut. ชาวบ้านพูด
The villagers are talking (gossiping).

74 THĂAM ถาม to ask (a question)

Khun Nók thăam wâa rau jà' maa mêua-rai.
คุณนกถามว่าเราจะมาเมื่อไหร่
Nok asked when we would come.

Thăam wâa... ถามว่า May I ask...

Jerry thăam wâa rau mii wehlaa rěu bplàu.
เจอรี่ ถามว่าเรามีเวลาหรือเปล่า
Jerry asked whether (if) we have time or not.

Note: "if" in a conditional sense is **thâa** ถ้า, e.g. **Thâa yàang nán...** ถ้าอย่างนั้น If that's the case/in that case...

75 BPLAE แปล
1) to mean (by explanation, translation);
2) to translate

Bplae wâa... แปลว่า That means, that is to say...

Nîi bplae wâa arai? นี่แปลว่าอะไร

What does this mean?

Chûay bplae jòtmǎai jàak faen.

ช่วย แปล จดหมาย จาก แฟน

Please help translate this letter from my girlfriend.

76 RÎAK เรียก 1) to be called; 2) to call

Khǒng níi rîak wâa arai. ของนี้เรียกว่าอะไร

What's this thing called?

Phonlamái níi rîak wâa mangkhút.

ผลไม้นี้เรียกว่ามังคุด

This fruit is called a mangosteen.

Rîak dtamrùat! เรียกตำรวจ Call the police!

77 KHÍT คิด to think, reckon, calculate

Khǎu khít wâa khon Thai jai dii mâak.

เขาคิดว่าคนไทยใจดีมาก

He thinks Thai people are very kind.

Khwaam khít ความคิด thought.

Khít lêhk คิดเลข
to do sums (literally "reckon figures")

Khít ngeun dûai. คิดเงินด้วย Check the bill, please.

Khít mâi òrk. คิดไม่ออก I can't figure it out.

Khít thĕung คิดถึง
thinking of you (missing you) (at end of a letter).

Lorng khít duu ลองคิดดู to think something over
Note: The word **lorng** ลอง means "to try out," so here, to try and see what something is like by thinking it over.

78 PHRÓ' เพราะ because, as

Tham-mai khun mâi maa? ทำไมคุณไม่มา
Why didn't you come?

→ **Phró' wâa leum.** เพราะว่า ลืม Because I forgot.

Rau jamdâi, phró' wâa sămkhan mâak.
เราจำได้ เพราะว่า สำคัญมาก
We remembered, because it is very important.

Jambpen dtông séu khâau, phró' wâa jà' mòt.

จำเป็นต้องซื้อข้าวเพราะว่าจะหมด

It's necessary to buy some rice, as it's going to run out.

Khun khruu dù', phró' wâa dèk-dèk son.

คุณครูดุ เพราะว่า เด็กๆ ซน

The teacher was cross because the children were naughty.

79 KHAM คำ word(s), speech

Grammatical note

This word often occurs as the first element in expressions that refer to what is uttered in words, e.g.:

Kham-khŏrthôot: คำขอโทษ apology

Kham-dù'dàa: คำดุด่า scolding, verbal abuse

Glàp-kham: กลับคำ to go back on one's word

Kham-bòn: คำบ่น complaint

Kham-sǎnyaa: คำสัญญา promise

And of course various grammatical terms, such as **kham-naam** กำนาม "noun," and **kham-griyaa** คำกริยา "verb."

80 GAMLANG กำลัง "in the process of"

Grammatical note
This word, when placed in front of a verb, indicates that the action is on-going, so we can translate it with the English present continuous tense.

Khun mâe gamlang khui gàp phêuan.
คุณแม่กำลัง คุย กับ เพื่อน
Mother is chatting with a friend.

Khun Manát gamlang thoh gàp nóng.
คุณ มนัส กำลัง โทรกับ น้อง
Mr Manat is on the phone with his (younger) brother/sister.

Note: The full term for "telephone" is **thohrasàp** โทรศัพท์, but this is generally shortened to just **thoh** โทร:

Thoh maa. โทรมา
There is a call for you (i.e. incoming).

Thoh bpai thĕung. โทรไปถึง
To call someone (i.e. outgoing).

PART 9

Words 81–90

Health and the body

81 BPÙAT ปวด to ache

Bpùat hǔa ปวด หัว (to have a) headache
thórng ปวดท้อง stomach-ache
fan ปวด ฟัน toothache
hǔu ปวด หู earache
lǎng ปวด หลัง backache

82 JÈP เจ็บ to hurt, be sore

Yàa tham, jèp! อย่าทำ เจ็บ Don't do that, it hurts!

Thâa jèp, bòrk ná? ถ้าเจ็บ บอกนะ
If it hurts, tell me, won't you.

Note: The little word **na** นะ, here with a high tone, can be called a particle, and it has the function of gentle urging: "okay?".

Jèp dtrong níi. เจ็บตรงนี้ It hurts here (pointing).

Jèp dtrong nǎi. เจ็บตรงไหน Where does it hurt?

Jèp khor เจ็บ คอ to have a sore throat.

83 BPEN เป็น to suffer (from an illness)

Bpen wàt เป็นหวัด to have a cold

Khau <u>bpen wàt</u>. เขาเป็นหวัด He has a cold.

Substitute the noun underlined:
Bpen khâi ไข้ to have a fever (temperature)
Bpen khâi wàt ไข้หวัด to have the flu
Bpen phlǎe แผล to have a wound (cut, sore place)
Bpen lom เป็น ลม to feel faint
Bpen rôhk AIDS โรคเอดส์ (pron. "ehd")
to have AIDS
Bpen rôhk phûu yǐng โรคผู้หญิง
to suffer from an STD
Bpen maigren ไมเกรน to have a migraine headache
Bpen aesmâa แอชมา to have asthma

But the following phrases do not need **bpen**:
thórng deun ท้องเดิน to have a "running stomach"

thórng sǐa ท้องเสีย to have an upset stomach
thórng rûang ท้อง ร่วง to have diarrhea

84 AAGAAN อาการ symptom(s)

Aagaan bpen yaang-rai? อาการเป็นอย่างไร
What are the symptoms?

Aagaan mâi dii. อาการ ไม่ ดี
The symptoms don't look good.

Aajian อาเจียน vomiting (informal: **ûak** อ้วก)
Bpen khâi sǔung เป็นไข้ สูง high fever
Wian-hǔa เวียนหัว dizziness
Norn mâi láp นอน ไม่ หลับ Can't sleep
Gin ahǎan mâi dâi. กินอาหารไม่ได้
I can't eat. No appetite.
Ai ไอ Coughing

85 DTORN ตอน
part, section (of time or space)

Dtorn cháau ตอนเช้า in the morning

Dtorn cháau rau bpai hông-náam.
ตอนเช้าเราไปห้องน้ำ
In the morning we go to the bathroom (toilet).

Substitute the word underlined:

Gin aahǎan cháau กิน อาหาร เช้า have breakfast

Àap náam อาบน้ำ take a bath

Bpraeng fan แปรงฟัน clean our teeth

Wǐi phǒm หวีผม brush our hair

Dtàeng dtua แต่งตัว get dressed

Hǎa wâen-dtaa หา แว่นตา

go looking for our glasses

Dtorn thîang rau bpai gin ahǎan-thîang.

ตอนเที่ยงเราไปกินอาหารเที่ยง

At noon we have lunch.

Dtorn bàai rau bpai gin ahǎan-wâang.

ตอนบ่าย เรา ไป กิน อาหารว่าง

In the afternoon we have a snack.

Dtorn yen rau bpai gin ahǎan yen.

ตอนเย็นเราไปกินอาหารเย็น

In the evening we eat dinner.

Dtorn dèuk rau bpai disago. ตอนดึก เรา ไป ดิสโก

In the dead of night we go to a disco.

86 SǓAN-DTUA ส่วนตัว personal

Khǒrng chái sùan-dtua ของใช้ส่วนตัว
items for personal use (toiletries)

Dtriam khǒrng chái sùan-dtua gòrn bpai thîau
เตรียม ของใช้ ส่วนตัว ก่อน ไป เที่ยว
Preparation of personal items before we go on a trip:

Gradàat thít-chûu: กระดาษทิชชู
toilet paper (not "tissue paper"!)
Sabùu: สบู่ soap
Yaa sǐi fan: ยาสีฟัน toothpaste
Chaempuu: แชมพู shampoo
Bpâeng: แป้ง powder
Thǔng yaang: ถุงยาง condoms ("rubber bags")

87 YAA ยา medicine; drugs

Chìit yaa ฉีดยา to inject a drug or medicine

Yaa mét ยาเม็ด tablet, pill

Bai sàng yaa ใบสั่งยา prescription

Yaa thàay ยาถ่าย laxative

Yaa bâa ยาบ้า amphetamines

Yaa sùup ยา สูบ tobacco

Mau yaa เมายา drugged, doped

88 DTÌT ติด stuck, attached, addicted

Dtìt yaa ติดยา to be addicted to drugs

Dtìt lâu ติดเหล้า to be addicted to alcohol

Dtìt rôhk ติดโรค to catch a disease

Dtìt chéua ติดเชื้อ
to be infected (**chéua**: germ, bacteria)

Dtìt khúk ติดคุก to be in jail

Dtìt jai ติดใจ to be fond of, attracted by

Dtìt dtaam ติดตาม to follow, go in the tracks of

Rót dtìt รถติด a traffic-jam

89 NÛAT นวด massage

Hâi nûat ให้นวด to give a massage

Nûat bpàep boraan นวดแผนโบราณ old-style (traditional) Thai massage (no sex)

Chăn yàak hâi nûat nòi. ฉันอยากให้นวดหน่อย
I'd like (to be given) a massage.

Nûat lăng นวดหลัง to massage the back

90 HĂAI หาย to disappear; to get better

Hăai láew. หายแล้ว I'm better (the illness has gone).

Hăai bpùai rĕu yang? หาย ป่วย หรือ ยัง
Have you recovered from your sickness yet?

Hăai jèp măi? หายเจ็บไหม
Have you got over the soreness?

Wăen-dtaa hăai. แว่นตาหาย
My glasses have disappeared.

PART 10

Words 91–100

Going to the temple

Cultural Note

Thailand has thousands of Buddhist temples. This is because it is a Buddhist country. The kind of Buddhism is the same as that of Sri Lanka, Burma and Cambodia, that is, Theravada. The clergy (monks) wear distinctive yellow, orange or reddish brown robes and have shaven heads.

There are several large and famous temples in Bangkok that foreign visitors are often taken to see. You can admire the architecture and ornaments. There are also lesser known temples in the city that are worth seeing. Feel free to drop in—nobody will accost you! However, you are expected to observe the same rules as Thais do:

- remove your shoes before entering a building (the place to leave them will be clear, and is quite safe);
- dress respectfully—cover up the thighs and chest;
- if sitting on the floor, never point the feet in the direction of a Buddha image; and

- do not touch or climb on any Buddha image (photos are okay).

Thais are extremely sensitive about any intended or unintended disrespect toward the Buddhist religion, including Buddha images, large and small, because they are regarded as filled with sacred power (**saksit** ศักดิ์สิทธิ์).

By all means chat with a monk, if he wants to practice his English! You should greet him with a **waai** ไหว้, but he will not return it. (Monks only make a **waai** ไหว้ to their superiors.) A woman must never touch a monk, even his robe. This includes giving or receiving an object—it has to be put down first. This is because monks follow a very strict set of rules of life (called the **Vinaya** วินัย), which include chastity (not marrying or having any contact with females). They also never eat after midday, until the next morning, when they go out to collect alms in their bowl.

Supporting monks with donations of food, and similar acts of generosity, brings us religious merit (**bun** บุญ), which will help create good conditions for us in this life and the next. You may be interested to pick up a simple handbook of Buddhist belief and practice, including for example the Five Precepts:

1. I undertake the training in abstention from killing living beings;

2. I undertake the training in abstention from taking what is not given;
3. I undertake the training in abstention from acts of sexual misconduct;
4. I undertake the training in abstention from false speech;
5. I undertake the training in abstention from using any intoxication substance.

You will see that these are not formulated as "commandments," but are intended as guidelines for mindfulness, leading to wisdom. But by no means all Thai people stick strictly to these precepts!

The monks spend most of their time in the temple, where they chant (in Pali, the ancient language of the Buddha), hold ceremonies, preach to the lay people, study, or are available for consultation. They also go out, when invited, to hold ceremonies with chanting such as a house-warming in order to convey blessings for a new home or business. Some monks teach ethics in schools. Others devote their lives to contemplation and meditation.

91 **WÁT** วัด temple

Wát Phrá' Gâeo วัดพระแก้ว Temple of the Emerald
Buddha (in central Bangkok)

Wát Phoh วัดโพธิ์ Temple of the Reclining Buddha

Wát Baworn วัดบวร (also spelled **Bovornives**)
famous as seat of the Supreme Patriarch and for its
teaching and meditation program

Wát Arun วัดอรุณ Temple of the Dawn

Wát Phrá' Sïi Mahăathâat วัดพระศรีมหาธาตุ
name of the oldest temple in Nakhorn Si Thammarat in
southern Thailand

Wat Prathâat Doi Suthêhp พระธาตุดอยสุเทพ
name of the most famous temple of Chiangmai.

92 **PHRÁ'** พระ
1) title before sacred places, persons and
objects; 2) a monk

Phrá' Phútthajâau พระพุทธเจ้า Lord Buddha

Phrá' Jâau พระเจ้า God

Phrá' Yehsuu พระเยซู Jesus

Phrá' Jâau Yùu Hŭa พระเจ้าอยู่หัว
His Majesty the King

Phrá' Nakhorn พระนคร the capital city, Bangkok

Phrá' Raachawang พระราชวัง the Royal Palace

Phrá' Sangkharâat พระสังฆราช
the Supreme Patriarch (Sangharaja)

Phrá' phúttharûup พระพุทธรูป a Buddha image

Wan phrá' วันพระ
the four holy days in a (lunar) month

Phrá' khrêuang พระเครื่อง a holy amulet

Phrá' bprajam wan พระประจำวัน
the Buddha that presides over the day of the week on
which one was born.

93 **BUN** บุญ (religious) merit

Tham bun ทำบุญ
to make merit (e.g. by offering food to monks, giving to beggars, releasing birds and so on)

Tham bun <u>wan gèut</u> ทำบุญวันเกิด
to make merit on your birthday

Substitute the noun underlined:

khêun bâan mài ขึ้นบ้านใหม่
on entering a new home (house-warming)
wan dtàeng ngaan วันแต่งงาน on your wedding day
ngaan sòp งานศพ at a funeral

94 **SÀKSÌT** ศักดิ สิทธิ holy, sacred

Wát níi sàksìt. วัดนี้ ศักดิ์สิทธิ This temple is holy.

Phrá' phúttarûup sàksìt. พระพุทธรู ศักดิ์สิทธิ
The Buddha image is sacred.

Phrá' khrêuang sàksìt พระเครื่อ ศักดิ์สิทธิ์
a holy amulet.

Khon Thai buuchaa sìng sàksìt.
คนไทยบูชาสิ่งศักดิ์สิทธิ์
The Thais venerate holy objects.

Dtônmái sàksìt ต้นไม้ศักดิ์สิทธิ a holy tree

95 SĬIN ศีล moral precept

Phrá' mii sĭin 227 khôr. พระมีศีล 227 ข้อ
Monks have 227 precepts. (**khôr** ข้อ: item)

Nehn mii sĭin 10 khôr. เณรมีศีล 10 ข้อ
Novices have ten precepts.

Mâe chii mii sĭin 8 khôr. แม่ชีมีศีล 8 ข้อ
Nuns have eight precepts.

Khon Thai mii sĭin 5 khôr.
คนไทยมีศีล 5 ข้อ
Ordinary Thais have five precepts.

96 HÂAM ห้าม to forbid; to be forbidden

Phûu yĭng hâam jàp phrá'. ผู้หญิงห้ามจับพระ
Women are forbidden to touch a monk.

Hâam khâa sàt. ห้ามฆ่าสัตว์
It is forbidden to kill animals.

Hâam sòng sǐang dang. ห้าม ส่ง เสียง ดัง
It is forbidden to make a loud noise.

Hâam khâu. ห้ามเข้า No entry.

Hâam hâi ahǎan sàt. ห้ามให้อาหารสัตว์
It is forbidden to feed the animals.

Hâam thíng khayá'. ห้ามทิ้งขยะ
It is forbidden to litter (throw away rubbish).

97 RONGRIAN โรงเรียน school

Rongrian yùu glâi wát. โรงเรียนอยู่ใกล้วัด
The school is near the temple.

Mii rongrian yài yùu lǎng wát.
มีโรงเรียนใหญ่อยู่หลังวัด
There is a large school behind the temple.

Phrá' sǒn sǐinlatham thîi rongrian.
พระ สอนศีลธรรมที่โรงเรียน
The monk teaches ethics at the school.

Rongrian bprathŏm โรงเรียนปรถม
primary school

Rongrian mátthayom โรงเรียนมัธยม
secondary school.

98 NĂNGSĔU หนังสือ book

Dèk rian năngsĕu thîi rongrian.
เด็กเรียนหนังสือที่โรงเรียน
The children study their books in the school.

Mii ráan năngsĕu khâng wát.   มีร้านหนังสือข้างวัด
There is a bookshop beside the temple.

Mii <u>năngsĕu phim</u> มี หนังสือพิมพ์.
They have <u>newspapers</u>.

Substitute the underlined word:
năngsĕu rian หนังสือเรียน textbooks
năngsĕu phrá' หนังสือ พระ religious books
năngsĕu dèk หนังสือเด็ก children's books
năngsĕu kaathuun หนังสือการ์ตูน comic books.

99 WAN วัน day

Wan gèut วันเกิด birthday

Wan yùt วันหยุด a holiday

Wan Phôr วันพ่อ "Father's Day," that is, the King's birthday, 5 December

Wan Mâe วันแม่
"Mother's Day," the Queen's birthday, 12 August

Wan Dèk วันเด็ก Children's Day

Wan Sŏngkhraan วันสงกรานต์
Songkran Day (variable date, in April)

100 RÊUK ฤกษ์ auspicious time

Rêuk dii ฤกษ์ ดี
the auspicious moment for something

Dâi rêuk ได้ ฤกษ์ to reach the auspicious time

Mŏr duu hâi rêuk dtàeng ngaan.

หมอดูให้ฤกษ์แต่งงาน

The fortune-teller gives a lucky time for the wedding.

Cultural note

Lucky days are calculated on the basis of the stars, that is, the various constellations in the sky, and it is the work of professional fortune-tellers to advise when it is propitious for a person to undertake some important task. Some monks also specialize in this.

English-Thai Wordlist

about, concerning, relating to **rêuang** เรื่อง

about, approximately (informal) **rau-rau** ราว ราว,
  (formal) **bpra-maan** ประมาณ

ache, to **bpùat** ปวด

addicted **dtìt** ติด

afternoon, in the **dtorn bàai** ตอนบ่าย

again, anew **mài** ใหม่,
  (another time) **ìik khráng** อีกครั้ง

age; to be aged… **aayú'** อายุ

AIDS **rôhk AIDS** โรคเอดส์ (pron. **ehd** เอด)

airport **sanǎam-bin** สนามบิน

alcohol, liquor **lâo** เหล้า

all, at all **leui** เลย

American **amerigan** อเมริกัน

amphetamines **yaa bâa** ยาบ้า

amulet **phrá' khrêuang** พระเครื่อง

and **láe'** และ

animal **sàt** สัตว์

another, more **ìik** อีก

anthem, national **phlehng châat** เพลงชาติ

any-, anything **arai gôr dâi** อะไรก็ได้;
  anyone **khrai gôr dâi** ใครก็ได้;
  any time **meua-rai gôr dâi** เมื่อไหร่ก็ได้;
  any kind **thúk yaang** ทุกอย่าง

apartment **apaatmen** อพาร์ตเม็น

apologize, to **khǒr thôht** ขอโทษ;

   apology **kham khǒr thôht** คำขอโทษ

apple **aepen** แอปเปิน

arrive, to **thěung** ถึง

article, thing, goods **khǒrng** ของ

ask, to (a question) **thǎam (wâa)** ถามว่า

asthma **aesmâa** แอสม่า

back (side) **khâng lǎng** ข้างหลัง;

   to go back, return **glàp** กลับ;

   to go back on one's word **glàp kham** กลับคำ

backache **bpùat lǎng** ปวดหลัง

bad **leho** เลว

bag (handbag, suitcase) **gra-bpǎu** กระเป๋า

bank (of river) **fàng (náam)** ฝั่งน้ำ

bank (for money) **thana-khaan** ธนาคาร

banknote **bank** แบงค์/ **thana-bat** ธนบัตร

  (counting word: **bai** ใบ)

bath, to take a bath **àap náam** อาบน้ำ

bathroom **hông-náam** ห้อง น้ำ

be, to (not translated in many cases);

   to be there, present **yùu** อยู่

beach **chaihàat** ชายหาด

beautiful **sǔai** สวย

because **phró' wâa** เพราะว่า

bed **dtiang** เตียง

beef **néua** เนื้อ

beer **bia** เบียร์

believe, to **chêua** เชื่อ;
   believable **nâa-chêua** น่าเชื่อ

beside **khâng** ข้าง

big **yài** ใหญ่

birthday **wan gèut** วันเกิด

bit, a **nít nòi** นิดหน่อย

black **sǐi dam** สีดำ

blouse **sêua phûu yǐng** เสื้อสีดำ

boat **reua** เรือ

book **nǎngsěu** หนังสือ

book, to **jorng** จอง

boring **nâa-bèua** น่าเบื่อ

born, to be **gèut** เกิด

boss, head **hǔa nâa** หัวหน้า

bottle **khwàt** ขวด

boxing **muay** มวย;
   boxer **nák-muay** นักมวย

boyfriend **faen** แฟน

breakfast **ahǎan cháau** อาหารเช้า

British **anggrìt** อังกฤษ

brother (older) **phîi** พี่; (younger) **nóng** น้อง

brothers and sisters (siblings) **phîi-nóng** พี่น้อง

brother-in-law (older) **phîi khěui** พี่เขย;
   (younger) **nóng khěui** น้องเขย

brush, to (hair) **wǐi** หวี

Buddha image **phrá' phúttharûup** พระพุทธรูป

bus **rót bas, rót meh** รถบัส รถเมล์

bus station **sathaanii rót bas** สถานีรถบัส

business **thurá'** ธุระ

buy, to **séu** ซื้อ

by (means of) **doi** โดย

calculate, to **khít** คิด

call, to; to be called **rîak (wâa)** เรียกว่า
   (*see also* telephone)

calm, cool-headed **jai-yen** ใจเย็น

can, able to **dâi** ได้

car **rót, rót yon** รถ รถยนต์

cash **ngeun sòt** เงินสด

cat **maeo** แมว

catch, to (a disease) **dtìt rôhk** ติดโรค

ceremony, festival, celebration **ngaan** งาน

change (small money) **ngeun thorn** เงินทอน

charter, to **mǎu** เหมา

chat, to **khui** คุย

cheap **thùuk** ถูก

cheap, easy to get (woman) **jai-ngâai** ใจง่าย

check (bank document) **chék** เช็ค

chicken **gài** ไก่

child (young person) **dèk** เด็ก; (someone's offspring)
   lûuk ลูก

chilli **phrík** พริก

Chinese **jiin** จีน

chopstick(s) **dtagìap** ตะเกียบ

clean (adjective) **sá-àat** สะอาด

clean, to (teeth) **bpraeng fan** แปรงฟัน

climate **aagàat** อากาศ

clinic **kliinik** คลีนิค

close **glâi** ใกล้

cloth **phâa** ผ้า

clothes **phâa** ผ้า

cloud **mêhk** เมฆ

coffee **gaafae** กาแฟ

cold **năau** หนาว

cold, to have a cold **bpen wàt** เป็นหวัด

color **sĭi** สี

come, to **maa** มา

comfortable **sabai** สบาย

comic book **năngsĕu khaa-thuun** หนังสือการ์ตูน

complain, to **bòn** บ่น;
    complaint **kham-bòn** คำ บ่น

completely **khròp** ครบ, **tháng-mòt** ทั้งหมด

compose, to (write, a song) **dtàeng phlehng** แต่งเพลง;
    composer, songwriter **nák dtàeng phlehng**
    นักแต่งเพลง

condominium **kondoh** คนโด; **hông-chút** ห้องชุด

consideration (for others) **greng-jai** เกรงใจ

consult, to (doctor, dentist) **hăa** หา

cook, to (prepare food) **tham ahăan** ทำอาหาร

correct, right **thùuk** ถูก

cotton cloth **phâa fâai** ผ้าฝ้าย

cough, to **ai** ไอ

cow **wua** วัว

credit card **bàt kredít** บัตรเครดิต

cross (angry) **grôht** โกรธ **mohǒ** โมโห

cross, to (street) **khâam** ข้าม

cry, to (weep) **rórng hâi** ร้องไห้

cry, to cry out **rórng** ร้อง

cup **thûai** ถ้วย

curry **gaeng** แกง

dance, to **dtênram** เต้นรำ;
   dancer **nák dtênram** นักเต้นรำ;
   classical Thai dance **ram Thai** รำไทย;
   folk dance (in circles) **ram wong** รำวง

daughter **lûuk sǎau** ลูกสาว

day **wan** วัน

deceased (to pass away) **sǐa chiiwít** เสียชีวิต

decorate, to **dtàeng** แต่ง

department, section **phanàek** แผนก

department store **depaatmensto** ดีพาร์ทเม็น สโต

dentist **mǒr fan** หมอฟัน

diarrhea **thórng deun/rûang** ท้องเดิน ท้องร่วง

die, to **dtai** ตาย

difficult **yâak** อยาก

dinner **ahǎan yen** อาหารเย็น

dirty **sòk-gà-bpròk** สกปรก

disappear, to **hǎai** หาย

disco **disko** ดีสโก

disease **rôhk** โรค

disheartened, to lose heart **jai-sǐa** ใจเสีย

district **ampheu (amphur)** อำเภอ

divorce, to; to be divorced **yàa** หย่า

dizzy **wian-hǔa** เวียนหัว

doctor **mǒr** หมอ

don't! **yàa** อย่า

double room **hông khûu** ห้องคู่;
    double bed **dtiang khûu** เตียงคู่

downstairs **khâng lâng** ข้างล่าง

dress, to get dressed **dtàeng-dtua** แต่งตัว

drink, to **deum** ดื่ม; **gin** (informal) กิน

drug **yaa** ยา

drugged, doped **mau yaa** เมายา

drunk **mau** เมา; **mau-lâu** เมาเหล้า

durian **thurian** ทุเรียน

each other **gan** กัน

earache **bpùat hǔu** ปวดหัว

easy **ngâai** ง่าย

eat, to **gin** กิน

edge (of river) **rim** ริม

egg **khài** ไข่

elephant **cháang** ช้าง

embassy **sathǎan thûut** สถานทูต

English (language) **phaasǎa anggrìt** ภาษาอังกฤษ

enjoy, to (oneself) **sanùk** สนุก

ethics, moral code **sǐinlatham** ศีลธรรม

ever **khoei** เคย

every **thúk** ทุก

everything **thúk yàang** ทุกอย่าง

exchange, to (money) **lâek** แลก

excited **jai-dtên** ใจเต้น; **dtèun-dtên** ตื่นเต้น

excuse me **khǒr thôht** ขอโทษ

exit **thaang òrk** ทางออก

expensive **phaeng** แพง

eye **dtaa** ตา

faint, to; to feel faint **bpen lom** เป็นลม

fall, to **dtòk** ตก

far **glai** ไกล

fare, rate, tariff **khâa** ค่า

father **phôr** พ่อ

father-in-law **phôr dtaa** พ่อตา (wife's father);
  phôr phǔa พ่อผัว (husband's father)

female **yǐng** หญิง

fever, to have a fever **bpen-khâi** เป็นไข้

finished (done) **sèt** เสร็จ; (used up) **mòt** หมด

fish **bplaa** ปลา

five **hâa** ห้า

floor (level) **chán** ชั้น

flu **khâi wàt** ไข้หวัด

follow, to **dtaam** ตาม

fond of, attracted to **dtìt jai** ติดใจ

food **ahǎan** อาหาร;

   Thai food **ahǎan Thai** อาหารไทย

football (soccer) **fútbon** ฟุตบอล

forbid, to; forbidden **hâam** ห้าม

foreigner (Westerner) **faràng** ฝรั่ง

forget, to **leum** ลืม

fortune-teller **mǒr duu** หมอดู

four **sìi** สี่

French **faràngsèt** ฝรั่งเศส

fried rice **khâau phàt** ข้าวผัด

friend **phêuan** เพื่อน;

   to be friends **bpen phêuan gan** เป็นเพื่อนกัน

from **jàak** จาก

front **khâng nâa** ข้างหน้า

fruit (in general) **phǒnlamái** ผลไม้

full, to have eaten enough **ìm** อิ่ม

fun, amusement, a good time **sanùk** สนุก

funny, comical **dtalòk** ตลก

funeral **ngaan sòp** งานศพ

German **yeraman** เยอรมัน

ghost **phǐi** ผี

girlfriend **faen** แฟน

give, to **hâi** ให้

glass **gâeu** แก้ว

glasses **wâen-dtaa** แว่นตา

go, to **bpai** ไป; to go up **khêun** ขึ้น;
   to go down **long** ลง

good **dii** ดี; goodness **khwaam dii** ความดี

goodbye **laa-gòr** ลาก่อน; **bai-bai** บายบาย;
   (sa)wàtdii สวัสดี

green **sǐi khǐau** สีเขียว

guitar **gii-dtâa** กีตาร์

hair **phǒm** ผม

half **khrêung** ครึ่ง

hand **meu** มือ

handsome **lòr** หล่อ

happy **dii jai** ดีใจ; **mii khaam-sùk** มีความสุข

hard (heavy, work) **nàk** หนัก; (difficult) **yâak** ยาก

have, to **mii** มี

he **khǎu** เขา

headache **bpùat hǔa** ปวดหัว

health, in good health **sabai dii** สบายดี

heart (anatomical) **hǔa-jai** หัวใจ

hello **(sa)wàtdii** สวัสดี

here **thîi nîi** ที่นี่

high **sǔung** สูง

holiday, trip **thîau** เที่ยว;
   (day with no work) **wan yùt** วันหยุด

holy, sacred **sàksìt** ศักดิ์สิทธิ์

home **bâan** บ้าน; at home **thîi bâan** ที่บ้าน;
   to go home **glàp bâan** กลับบ้าน
hospital **rohng phayabaan** โรงพยาบาล
hot (temperature) **rórn** ร้อน
hotel **rongraem** โรงแรม; **hoten** โฮเต็น
hour **chûa-mong** ชั่วโมง
house **bâan** บ้าน
how? **yangai** ยังไง (informal),
   yang-rai อย่างไร (formal)
how many? **gìi** กี่
hundred **róoi** ร้อย
hurt, to (sore) **jèp** เจ็บ
hurt, offended **jèp-jai** เจ็บใจ
husband (informal) **phŭa** ผัว; (formal) **săamii** สามี

I (man speaking) **phŏm** ผม;
   (woman speaking, informal) **chăn** ฉัน,
   (woman speaking, formal) **dichăn** ดิฉัน
ice **nám-khăeng** น้ำแข็ง
if **thâa** ถ้า
important **săm-khan** สำคัญ
in, inside **nai** ใน
incorrect, wrong **phìt** ผิด
infected **dtìt chéua** ติดเชื้อ
inject, to **chìit** ฉีด
installments, in **phòn sòng** ผ่อนส่ง
interested, absorbed (in) **sŏn-jai** สนใจ

interesting **nâa-sǒnjai** น่าสนใจ

invite, to **cheun** เชิญ

it (a specific thing) **man** มัน (otherwise not translated)

item **khôr** ข้อ

jail **khúk** คุก

Japanese **yîi-bpùn** ญี่ปุ่น

joke, to **phûut lên** พูดเล่น

kill, to **khâa** ฆ่า

kilo **gi-loh** กิโล

kilometer **gi-loh** กิโล, **gi-lohmét** กิโลเมตร

kind, sort, variety **yàang** อย่าง

kind(hearted) **jai dii** ดีใจ

kindly, please **garunaa** กรุณา

king **phrá' jâau yùu hǔa** พระเจ้าอยู่หัว ในหลวง

kitchen **khrua** ครัว

know, to (informal) **rúu** รู้; (formal) **sâap** ทราบ

know, to (be acquainted) **rúujàk** รู้จัก

knowledge **khwaam rúu** ความรู้

lane **soi** ซอย

language **phaasǎa** ภาษา

last (week etc.) **thîi láeu** ที่แล้ว

late (behind time) **cháa** ช้า

late (in the morning) **sǎi** สาย

late at night **dtorn dtèuk** ตอนดึก

laxative **yaa thàai** ยาถ่าย

leave, to (go out) **òrk** ออก (from: **jàak** จาก)

left (hand) **sáai** สาย

let's go! **bpai!** ไป; **bpai-gan-theu** ไปกันเถอะ

letter **jòtmăai** จดหมาย

level (floor) **chán** ชั้น

lie down, to **norn** นอน

lift (elevator) **líp** ลิบ

like, similar **mĕuan** เหมือน

like, to; have a liking for **chôrp** ชอบ

like that, in that way **yàang nán** อย่างนั้น;
   like this **yàang níi** อย่างนี้

listen, to (to) **fang** ฟัง

little, small **lék** เล็ก

little, a little **nòi** หน่อย

live, to; to be at a location, dwell **yùu** อยู่

long (time) **naan** นาน

look, to look after, care for **duu lae** ดูแล;
   to look for **hăa** หา

lot, a lot of **yéuk** เยอะ (informal);
   mâak มาก (formal)

loud **dang** ดัง

love **rák** รัก

lovely, cute, attractive **nâa-rák** น่ารัก

luck, good **chohk dii** โชคดี

lunch **ahăan thîang** อาหารเที่ยง

lyrics (words of song) **néua phlehng** เนื้อเพลง

make, to **tham** ทำ

make-up, to put on make-up **dtàeng nâa** แต่งหน้า

male **chaai** ชาย

mango **ma-mûang** มะม่วง

mangosteen **mang-khút** มังคุด

many, several, various **lǎi** หลาย

market **dta-làat** ตลาด

marry, to; to be married **dtàeng-ngaan**
  (to: **gàp**) แต่งงานกับ

massage **nûat** นวด

may I have... **khǒr** ขอ

mean, to mean **bplae (wâa)** แปลว่า

mean, selfish **jai-dam** ใจดำ

medicine **yaa** ยา

medium (not too much) **bpaan-glaang** ปานกลาง

meet, to meet **phóp** พบ

meeting, conference **bpra-chum** ประชุม

melody, tune **thamnorng phlehng** ทำนองเพลง

menu **menu** เมนู

merit (religious) **bun** บุณ

middle, center **glaang** กลาง

migraine **maigren** ไมเกรน

milk **nom** นม

minute **naathii** นาที

miss, to (think of) **khít thěung** คิดถึง

miss (title) **naang sǎau** นางสาว

moment, auspicious **rêuk** ฤกษ์

money **ngeun** เงิน

monk **phrá'** พระ

month **deuan** เดือน

morning **dtorn cháau** ตอนเช้า

most, the (-est) **thîi sùt** ที่สุด

mother **mâe** แม่

mother-in-law (wife's mother) **mâe yaai** แม่ยาย;
  (husband's mother) **mâe phǔa** แม่ผัว, **mâe sǎamii**
  แม่สามี

motorcycle **motersai** มอเตอร์ไซ จักรยานยนต์

mountain **phu-khǎu** ภูเขา

movie, film **nǎng** หนัง;
  movie theater **rohng nǎng** โรงหนัง

much, a lot, very **mâak** มาก

museum **phi-phít-ta-phan** พิพิธภัณฑ์

music **don-dtrii** ดนตรี

name **chêu** ชื่อ;
  family name **naam sagun** นามสกุล;
  first name **chêu jing** ชื่อจริง;
  nickname **chêu lên** ชื่อเล่น

nation, nationality; national **châat** ชาติ

naughty **son** ซน

necessary **jam-bpen** จำเป็น

need, to **dtông** ต้อง;
  no need **mâi dtông** ไม่ต้อง

neighbor **phêuan bâan** เพื่อนบ้าน

new **mài** ใหม่

newspaper **năngsĕu phim** หนังสือพิมพ์

night, at night **glaang kheun** กลางคืน

no (I don't agree) **mâi châi** ไม่ใช่;
  (I don't want it) **mâi au** ไม่เอา

noon, at noon **dtorn thîang** ตอนเที่ยง

north-east **isăan** อิสาน

not **mâi** ไม่

not very **mâi khôi** ไม่ค่อย

novice (Buddhist) **nehn** เณร

number (in street; telephone) **ber** เบอร์;
  (figure) **lêhk** เลข

nun **mâe chii** แม่ชี

object, thing **sìng** สิ่ง

office **óp-fít** อ๊อบฟิต

old-fashioned, traditional **bo-raan** โบราณ

on (on top of) **bon** บน

one **nèung** หนึ่ง

or **rĕu** หรือ; or not **rĕu bplàu** หรือเปล่า

palace, royal **phrá' raa-cha-wang** พระราชวัง

pants, trousers **gang-gehng** กางเกง

paper **gra-dàat** กระดาษ

parents **phôr-mâe** พ่อแม่

passport **năngsĕu deun thaang** หนังสือเดินทาง

pay, to **jàai** จ่าย

people **khon** คน

per, by the… **lá'** ละ

perform, to; to show, display
sa-daeng แสดง

performance, exhibition **gaan sa-daeng** การแสดง

performer **phûu sa-daeng** ผู้แสดง

person **khon** คน

personal **sǔan dtua** ส่วนตัว

pick up, to (take) **gèp** เก็บ; (go and meet) **ráp** รับ

pig **mǔu** หมู

place **thîi** ที่;
place to sit **thîi nâng** ที่นั่ง

plane **khrêuang bin** เครื่องบิน

plate **jaan** จาน

play, drama **la-khorn** ละคร

play, to **lên** เล่น

pleased, glad **yin dii** ยินดี

pleased, delighted **cheun-jai** ชื่นใจ

poet **ga-wii** กวี

police station **sa-thǎa-nii dtam rùat** สถานี ตำรวจ

pork **mǔu** หมู

pot (for rice) **môr** หม้อ

powder (talcum) **bpaeng** แป้ง

precept, moral **sǐin** ศีล

pregnant **mii thórng** มี ท้อง

prescription (for medicine) **bai sàng yaa** ใบสั่งยา

price **raa-khaa** ราคา

primary (school) **bpra-thǒm** ประถม
province **jangwàt (changwat)** จังหวัด
put, to put in, add **sài** ใส่
pyjamas **chút norn** ชุดนอน

quarrel, to **thaló' gan** ทะเลาะกัน
queen **phrá' raa-chi-nii** พระราชินี

rain **fǒn** ฝน
reach, to **thǔeng** ถึง
really (believe me!) **jing-jing!** จริง จริง
reasonable **mo'sǒm** เหมาะสม
recover, to (from illness) **hǎai** หาย
red **sǐi daeng** สีแดง
reduce, to (lower) **lót** ลด
region (of Thailand) **phâak** ภาค
religious book **nǎngsǔeu phrá'** หนังสือพระ
remember, to **jamdâi** จำได้
remove, to (take off, clothes, shoes) **thòrt** ถอด
rent, to **châu** เช่า
reserve, to **jorng** จอง
restaurant **ráan ahǎan** ร้านอาหาร
retail **bplìik** ปลีก
return, to (go back) **glàp** กลับ;
    out and back **bpai-glàp** ไป กลับ
rice **khâau** ข้าว;
    sticky rice **khâau nǐau** ข้าวเหนียว

rice field **naa** นา

rich **ruai** รวย

right (hand) **kwǎa** ขวา

right here/there **dtrong níi** ตรงนี้; **dtrong-nán** ตรงนั้น

river **mâe-náam** แม่น้ำ

road **tha-nǒn** ถนน

roast, roast chicken **gài yâang** ไก่ย่าง

room **hông** ห้อง;
   single room **hông dîau** ห้องเดี่ยว;
   double room **hông khûu** ห้องคู่

rubbish **khayá'** ขยะ

run, to **wîng** วิ่ง

run, to run out of something **mòt** หมด; **mâi mii láeu** ไม่มีแล้ว

sauce, dip **nám jîm** น้ำจิ้ม

say, to **bòrk** บอก

scary, frightening **nâa-glua** น่ากลัว

school **rong-rian** โรงเรียน

scolding, (verbal) abuse **kham-dù' dàa** คำดุด่า

seat **thîi nâng** ที่นั่ง

secondary (school) **matthayom** มัธยม

sell, to **khǎi** ขาย

separate, to; to be separated **yâek** แยก

shampoo **chaem-phuu** แชมพู; **yaa sà' phǒm** ยาสระผม

she **khǎu** เขา; **lòn** หล่อน

shoe(s) **rorng tháau** รองเท้า

shop **ráan** ร้าน

show **shoh** โชว์; **gaan sa-daeng** การแสดง

sick, to be sick **bpùai** ป่วย; **mai sabai** ไม่สบาย

side **khâng** ข้าง

side-street **soi** ซอย

silk cloth **phâa mǎi** ผ้าไหม

sincere, heartfelt **jing-jai** จริงใจ

sing, to sing (a song) **rórng phlehng** ร้องเพลง

singer **nák rórng** นักร้อง

single, sole **dîau** เดี่ยว;
   single room **hông dîau** ห้องเดี่ยว;
   single bed **dtiang dîau** เตียงเดี่ยว

single, unmarried **bpen sòht** เป็นโสด

sister (older) **phîi** พี่;
   (younger) **nóng** น้อง

sister-in-law (older) **phîi saphái** พี่สะใภ้;
   (younger) **nóng saphái** น้อง สะใภ้

size **kha-nàat** ขนาด

skilled, good at something **gèng** เก่ง

skin **pyǔ** ผิว

skirt **grà-bprohng** กระโปรง

skytrain **rót fai fáa** รถไฟฟ้า

slander, gossip **nin-thaa** นินทา

sleep, to **làp** หลับ

slowly **cháa-cháa** ช้า ช้า

small **lék** เล็ก

smelly **měn** เหม็น

snack, to have a snack **gin lên** กินเล่น

snake **nguu** งู

snooze, to **norn lên** นอนเล่น

soap **sabùu** สบู่

sometimes **baang thii** บางที

son **lûuk chaai** ลูกชาย

sound, noise **sǐang** เสียง

south **dtâi** ใต้

speak, to **phûut** พูด

spoon **chórn** ช้อน

sportsman/woman **nák gilaa** นัก กิฬา

stairs **bandai** บันได

station **sathǎanii** สถานี;
   railway station **sathǎanii rót fai** สถานีรถไฟ;
   bus station **sathǎanii rót bus** สถานีรถบัส

STD **rôhk phûu yǐng** โรคผู้หญิง

steak **sadték** สเต็ก

step- **lîang** เลี้ยง; step child **lûuk lîang** ลูกเลี้ยง

stomach-ache **bpùat thórng** ปวดท้อง

story, tale, subject, matter **rêuang** เรื่อง

straight on (ahead) **dtrong bpai** ตรงไป

stroll, to **deun lên** เดินเล่น

study, to **rian** เรียน

style **bàep** แบบ

sub-district **dtambon (tambon)** ตำบล

suffer, to (from illness) **bpen...** เป็น

sugar **nám-dtaan** น้ำตาล

sums, to do (calculate figures) **khít lêhk** คิดเลข

supper **ahǎan khâm** อาหารค่ำ

sweetheart **wǎan-jai** หวานใจ; **khon rák** คนรัก

symptom **aagaan** อาการ

table **dtó'** โต๊ะ

tablet, pill **yaa mét** ยาเม็ด

take, to take along, accompany **phaa** พา;
  pick up **gèp** เก็บ

take, to (time) **gin** กิน

take, to (accept) **au** เอา

talk, to **phûut** พูด

tasty (tempting to eat) **nâa-gin** กิน

taxi **rót táeksîi** รถแท็กซี่

tea **chaa** ชา

teach, to **sǒn** สอน

teacher (school) **khruu** ครู;
  (academic, religious) **ajaan** อาจารย์

telephone **thoh-rasàp** โทรศัพท์; **thoh** โทร;
  to telephone someone **thoh bpai hǎa** โทรไปหา;
  there is a telephone call **thoh maa** โทรมา

tell, to **bòrk** บอก

temple **wát** วัด

ten thousand **mèun** หมื่น

textbook **nǎngsěu rian** หนังสือ เรียน; **tamraa** ตำรา

than, compared with **gwàa** กว่า

thanks! **khorp-jai!** ขอบใจ (to a younger person)

that (one) **nán** นั้น; (after verbs of saying etc.) **wâa** ว่า

there **thîi nân** ที่ นั้น

they (people only) **khǎu** เขา

think, to **khít** คิด; to think over **khít duu** คิดดู

thirsty **hǐu náam** หิวน้ำ

this (one) **níi** นี้

thoughtfulness, goodwill **nám-jai** น้ำใจ

thousand **phan** พัน

three **sǎam** สาม

throat **khor** คอ

throw, to (away, out) **thíng** ทิ้ง

ticket **dtǔa** ตั๋ว

tie **nékthai** เน็คไท

time (length of) **wehlaa** เวลา;
  (occurrence) **khráng** ครั้ง;
  on time **dtrong wehlaa** ตรงเวลา;
  all the time **dta-lòrt wehlaa** ตลอดเวลา

timetable **dtaraang wehlaa** ตารางเวลา

tired **nèuai** เหนื่อย

title (name of story) **chêu rêuang** ชื่อเรื่อง

to (going toward) **bpai** ไป

tobacco **yaa sùup** ยาสูบ

today **wan níi** วันนี้

together **gan** กัน

toilet **hông-náam** ห้อง น้ำ

toilet paper **gradàat thít-chûu** กระดาษ ทิชชู่;
   gradàat chamrá' กระดาษชำระ

tomorrow **phrûng níi** พรุ่งนี้

too (excessively) **gern-bpai** เกินไป

tooth **fan** ฟัน

toothache **bpùat fan** ปวดฟัน

toothpaste **yaa sǐi fan** ยาสีฟัน

touch, to; grasp **jàp** จับ

traffic jam **rót dtìt** รถติด

train **rót fai** รถไฟ

translate, to **bplae** แปล

tree **dtôn mái** ต้นไม้

trip, excursion (to go on a trip) **bpai thîau** ไปเที่ยว

trusted, trusted friend **phêuan khûu-jai** เพื่อนคู่ใจ

try, to try out **lorng** ลอง

t-shirt **sêua yêut** เสื้อยืด

turn, to (in another direction) **líau** เลี้ยว

two **sǒng** สอง

under (below) **dtâi** ใต้

underground railway **rót fai dtâi din** รถไฟใต้ดิน

understand, to **khâu-jai** เข้าใจ

unmarried **bpen sòht** เป็นโสด

upper (level) **chán bon** ชั้นบน

upset stomach **thórng sǐa** ท้องเสีย

upstairs **khâng bon** ข้างบน

use, to **chái** ใช้

venerate, to (worship) **buu-chaa** บูชา

very, very much **mâak** มาก; **yeu'** เยอะ

village **mùu-bâan** หมู่บ้าน

villager **chaau bâan** ชาวบ้าน

vomit, to (informal) **ûak** อ้วก;

  (formal) **aajian** อาเจียน

wake up, to; to get up **dtèun** ตื่น

walk, to **deun** เดิน

want, to want to **yàak** อยาก

wash, to (clothes) **sák** ซัก

watch, to; to look at **duu** ดู

way (route; method) **thaang** ทาง;

  way out, exit **thaang òrk** ทางออก

we **rau** เรา

week **athít** อาทิตย์

well, healthy **sabai dii** สบายดี

what? **arai?** อะไร

when? **mêua-rai?** เมื่อไหร่

where? **thîi năi?** ที่ไหน

which? (of several things) **năi?** ไหน

white **sĭi khăau** สีขาว

wholesale **sòng** ส่ง

wife (informal) **mia** เมีย;

  (formal) **phanrayaa** ภรรยา;

  (minor wife, mistress) **mia nói** เมียน้อย

wind **lom** ลม

with **gàp** กับ
with, by **doi** โดย
word **kham** คำ
work, to **tham ngaan** ทำงาน
wound (cut, sore place) **phlăe** แผล

year **bpii** ปี
yesterday **mêua waan níi** เมื่อวานนี้
you (polite) **khun** คุณ; (intimate) **ther** เธอ;
　(respectful) **thâan** ท่าน

Appendices

Telling the time

Unfortunately, the common method of telling the time in Thai is rather complicated. The hours are as follows:

1 a.m. **dtii nèung** ตีหนึ่ง
2 a.m. **dtii sŏng** ตีสอง
3 a.m. **dtii săam** ตีสาม
4 a.m. **dtii sìi** ตีสี่
5 a.m. **dtii hâa** ตีห้า

6 a.m. **hòk mohng cháu** หกโมงเช้า
7 a.m. **jèt mohng cháu** เจ็ดโมงเช้า
8 a.m. **bpàet mohng cháu** แปดโมงเช้า
9 a.m. **gâu mohng cháu** เก้าโมงเช้า
10 a.m. **sìp mohng cháu** สิบโมงเช้า
11 a.m. **sìp-èt mohng cháu** สิบเอ็ดโมงเช้า

12 noon **thîang** เที่ยง

1 p.m. **bàai mohng** บ่ายโมง
2 p.m. **bàai sŏng mohng** บ่ายสองโมง
3 p.m. **bàai săam mohng** บ่ายสามโมง

4 p.m. **bàai sìi mohng** บ่ายสี่โมง or
sìi mohng yen สี่โมงเย็น

5 p.m. **hâa mohng** ห้าโมง or
hâa mohng yen ห้าโมงเย็น

6 p.m. **hòk mohng yen** หกโมงเย็น

7 p.m. **thûm** or **nèung thûm** ทุ่ม หนึ่งทุ่ม

8 p.m. **sŏng thûm** สองทุ่ม

9 p.m. **săam thûm** สามทุ่ม

10 p.m. **sìi thûm** สี่ทุ่ม

11 p.m. **hâa thûm** ห้าทุ่ม

12 midnight **thîang kheun** เที่ยงคืน

For the minutes after the hour, just add .... **naathii**
นาที

The 24-hour clock is also used for official purposes.
In this system the number of hours is followed by
naaligaa นาฬิกา, and the minutes after the hour by
naathii นาที (as above).

Days of the week

Monday **wan jan** วันจันทร์
Tuesday **wan angkhaan** วันอังคาร
Wednesday **wan phút** วันพุธ
Thursday **wan phareuhát** วัน พฤหัส

Friday **wan sùk** วันศุกร์
Saturday **wan săo** วันเสาร์
Sunday **wan aathít** วันอาทิตย์

Months of the year

January **mok-ga-raa-khom** มกราคม
February **gum-phaa-phan** กุมภาพันธ์
March **mii-naa-khom** มีนาคม
April **meh-săa-yon** เมษายน
May **phréut-saphaa-khom** พฤษภาคม
June **mí-thu-naa-yon** มิถุนายน
July **ga-rak-ga-daa-khom** กรกฎาคม
August **sĭng-hăa-khom** สิงหาคม
September **gan-yaa-yon** กันยายน
October **dtu-laa-khom** ตุลาคม
November **phréut-sa-ji-gaa-yon** พฤศจิกายน
December **than-waa-khom** ธันวาคม

Thai kinship terms

Father: **phôr** พ่อ
Mother: **mâe** แม่
Aunt (younger sister of mother): **náa** น้า
Aunt (younger sister of father): **aa** อา
Aunt (older sister of mother or father): **bpâa** ป้า
Uncle (younger brother of mother): **náa** น้า

Uncle (younger brother of father): **aa** อา
Uncle (older brother of father or mother): **lung** ลุง
Nephew: **lǎan-chai** หลานชาย
Niece: **lǎan sǎau** หลานสาว
Grandmother (paternal): **yâa** ย่า
Grandmother (maternal): **yaai** ยาย
Grandfather (paternal): **bpùu** ปู่
Grandfather (maternal): **dtaa** ตา
Grandchild: **lǎan** หลาน

Some Thai proverbs

1. **Deun dtaam naai, mǎa mâi gàt**
   เดินตามนาย หมาไม่กัด
   "If you follow the master, dogs won't bite you."
In other words: If you do what you're told, you'll be okay. This alludes to the system of hierarchy in Thai society, and the demands for conformity to rules and regulations; the authorities will block you if you don't toe the line. If you have conflict you won't get anywhere. Underlings, no matter how well qualified, have to do what the bosses demand.

2. **Àap náam rórn maa gorn** อาบน้ำร้อนมาก่อน
   "To take a warm bath before you."
In other words: I was born before you, so I have more experience than you, and you had better take my word

for it. Trust me! This is a bit like the English "I've had more hot dinners than you."

3. **Mái glâai fàng** ไม้ใกล้ฝั่ง
   "The log is near the bank."

In other words, my life is approaching its end (I have one foot in the grave), so you have to stand on your own feet, prepare yourself, set yourself up and get serious with your life. The image is of timber seasoning in a canal; if it is near the bank, it will soon be pulled out to be dried and milled.

4. **Măa gàt, yàa gàt dtòrp** หมากัดอย่ากัดตอบ
   "When the dog bites, don't bite back."

In other words: don't lower yourself to fight with someone else, or don't stoop as low as your enemy. Don't bother to argue back. Note that the dog is an image of something low; the same applies to most animals, which are born in that state because of a lack of good deeds in former lives.

5. **Lûuk mái lòn mâi glai dtôn**
   ลูกไม้หล่นไม่ไกลต้น
   "The fruit does not fall far from the tree."

English: Like father, like son.

6. **Duu cháang, hâi duu hăang; duu naang hâi duu mâe**
ดูช้างให้ดูหาง ดูนางให้ดูแม่

"Looking at an elephant, you should check its tail, and when looking at a girl, you should check her mother."

In other words, "like mother, like daughter."

7. **Jàp bplaa sŏng meu** จับปลาสองมือ

"Catching fish with two hands."

This means catching one fish in each hand, and losing both. In other words, it is better to focus on what you are doing, and do it well.

Emergency expressions

Sorry! (also: excuse me, pardon?)
Khŏr thôht ขอโทษ

Help! **Chûai dûai!** ช่วยด้วย

Fire! **Fai mâi!** ไฟไหม้

Police! **Dtamrùat! Dtamrùat!** ตำรวจ

Thief! **Khamoi!** ขโมย

Look out! (beware): **Rawang!** ระวัง

Don't (do that): **Yàa!** อย่า

Just a moment! **Dĭau gòrn.** เดี๋ยวก่อน

No! (that's not right): **Mâi châi!** ไม่ใช่

Stop! **Yùt!** หยุด

That's enough! **Pho láeu.** พอแล้ว

What a pity! **Sĭa dai.** เสียดาย

It's okay (I don't mind): **Mâi bpen rai.** ไม่เป็นไร

Thanks a lot! **Khop khun mâak!** ขอบคุณมาก

Right! (correct) **Châi!** ใช่

That's great! **Dii mâak!** ดีมาก

What fun! **Sanùk!** สนุก

That's odd! **Bplàek!** แปลก

What does… mean? **…. Bplae wâa arai?** แปลว่าอะไร

See you again! **Phóp gan mài.** พบกันใหม่

Suggestions for Further Reading

Becker, Benjawan Poomsan: *Thai for Beginners*. Bangkok & Berkeley: Paiboon Publishing, 1995

Becker, Benjawan Poomsan: *Thai-English English-Thai Dictionary* (with transliteration for non-Thai speakers) (fourth revision). Bangkok & Berkeley: Paiboon Publishing, 2002.

Golding, Michael & Benjawan Jai-Ua: *Essential Thai Phrase Book*. Singapore: Periplus, 2004.

Haas, Mary R.: *Thai-English Student's Dictionary*. Stanford: Stanford U.P. 1964.

Lonely Planet Phrasebooks and Bruce Evans: *Thai* (5th edition). Footscray: Lonely Planet, September 2004.

Robertson G. (compilor); Golding, Michael & Benjawan Jai-Ua (editors): *Robertson's Practical English–Thai Dictionary*. Singapore: Tuttle, 2004.

Wyatt, David, K.: *Thailand, A Short History*. New Haven & London: Yale U.P. 1984.